Kaostar!

...being the most Marvellous 'New Traditional' Sorcerous Magickal Rites of the Chaos Cunner and the Hideous Public Secrets of the Urbane Shaman

As related to his scribe by the venerable

Francis H Breakspear

Edited by Dave Evans

Written by Francis H Breakspear, edited by Dave Evans.

Published by Hidden Publishing
ISBN 978-0-9555237-1-7

Made in England, designed to be enjoyed anywhere.

The authors can be contacted care of here
katehoolu@yahoo.co.uk

Kaostar is a carbon-neutral title but we have variable attitudes to the other elements of the Periodic table

Contents

About the Author

Francis Breakspear was born in England and has been practising various kinds of magic (including the methods in this book) for well over two decades. This is his first print book.

By way of an introduction

The exact tale of the genesis of this book is a story that is probably longer than the actual book itself - suffice to say that many folk have been instrumental in the inspiration of the writing, and on those occasions when that inspiration has been of a positive nature and not simply indicating the best way to do something by their setting a really very bad and opposite example, our play at magick with them has on the whole been delightful, instructional, effective and deliciously entertaining in the extreme.

Our thanks to you all, especially to the mighty Ramsey Dukes (we are simply not worthy!), the intergalactic membership, if not any of the earthly representatives, of the *Syncretic Order of the Golden Giraffe*, to whom we raise a (top secret) salute, the *Church of the Flying Spaghetti Monster*, and to the utterly beautiful and completely magickal Transylvanian Lizard Queen, to whom we owe so much love that it actually hurts.

they are massing, on the wing
Swallows
"one Swallow doesn't make a summer"
well, it depends what you are prepared to swallow
but Swallows on the wing, massing
that means only one thing
no Swallows makes for winter

Francis Breakspear xx

Deep in 'The Sacred Groves', England,
Autumn 2006 e.v

The Real Introduction

Chaos Cunning Craft? What's that? Be patient for a moment please... we get there is a few pages. First, Chaos Magic(k)....

It is our opinion that *the nebulous, often ill-described and usually* dubiously sensationalised practices generically known as Chaos magick should be all about 'getting out there and doing it'. Sometimes it is also all about thinking about how to do it, and thus creatively inventing marvellous and sometimes scary new ways of how to do it. And *then* damn well doing it!

So this book has numerous parts that are conspicuously light on theory and/or pontification and very heavy on the practical side. This strategy is specifically for those who wish to skip the scene-setting or any hint of mysticism, philosophy, theoretical justifications or complex mathematics, and just go directly to getting up to their elbows (and-or genitals) right away in what is commonly referred to these days as 'results magick'. Which term begs the obvious question, what is this to differentiate it from... 'no-results magick' perhaps?

So to prevent having to go over the basics in great detail here and thus delay the actual practice (plus killing a few more trees in the process of adding pages to the print run) it is assumed of the reader that they already have at least a clue about, and some kind of grounding in how to actually 'do' magick in the first place.

This might be a manifestly dangerous assumption on our part, in which case please ensure that a 'responsible adult' (however you personally define that profoundly contentious term) is at hand if you are going to be working these spells as a complete beginner. They will actually work really well for someone with less presumptions, hang-ups and general egotism about their abilities and general importance in the world than any 'old hands'. To this end we have also assumed that you know what a banishing ritual is, and have made up your own mind about when and if such things need to be used; thus such preliminary matters are not discussed in any great length here.

For the most part the book need not be read in any linear fashion, so feel free to browse and dip in and out as you wish- treat it like a cookery book with various discrete recipes, not a novel or a sequential textbook which has a structure that must be followed, or stringently adhered to.

Some parts may not be to your taste at all, in which cases please do skip them, and where something is a follow-on discussion or method related to or derived from a previous piece then that is mentioned. As this is not intended as a shelf-reference book but rather a text to be used practically, there is no index. Due to this, please feel free to annotate, bend, fold, rip or generally mutilate the book, as you need, in order to make bookmarks.

The various techniques and rituals described here are all, for the most part, tested unless we say otherwise. They are also 'descriptive rather than prescriptive'; in other words, they are accounts of some rituals and methods performed, often written in a 'do this, then do that' format. However, being not Gurus who are remotely keen on gathering a following of thought-free uniformly drooling acolytes, we are not insisting that you are a sheep and exactly follow our acts in slavish fashion, but instead, like a really good cook using someone else's recipe book, you may choose to modify one, some or all details as you will, and learn in the process, much as we have done in designing and performing these rituals (or in some cases passing them on, somewhat adapted, from older and often very diverse sources).

Having said that, most of the material here comes from no recognised 'magickal tradition' that can be dated with any degree of reliability-credibility and without insincere laughter. Apart from some common household items and occasional things found out in the world it generally requires nothing but your mind and time (this is also known in some quarters as 'open handed magick').

We do not require you to as a qualifier to have been born within spitting distance of the grave of a mediaeval priest who allegedly died of a mysterious curse, or the site of a witch-burning in 1588, to be able to claim some faux-hereditary link to a famous magician, or whatever.

There are some elements herein that are 'kitchen-witchery' (magick relying on adapting 'normal' household materials), which is very much 'old-school cunning', truly resourceful and creative magic, and some of the suggested rituals require you to actually fabricate things beforehand, be they ritual tools or other items which are useful for the procedure. However the raw materials can be obtained from easy-to-find shops quite easily, and do not require you to travel the globe seeking out the perfect black egg of some rare Guatemalan snake and the left kidney of a virgin albino Yak that has been fed only on coconuts and Mung beans for 3 lunar cycles as vital pre-cursor item before you can start even a basic conjuration.

Be prepared to learn how to use a pair of scissors, a needle and thread, glue, spray paint and occasionally such things as a power drill, if you have not already some competence with those items. Those are all impeccable and powerful magical weapons, when wielded well, and with the correct focused intent.

There will also be a few of these boxes scattered around the book:

> **Handy Hint:**
>
> You will find a fair need for 6 inch nails in many of the spells herein, so buy a large box of the things next time you are in a hardware store and carry a couple with you wherever possible, if you can't find some meaty-looking old ones to recycle, see image below.

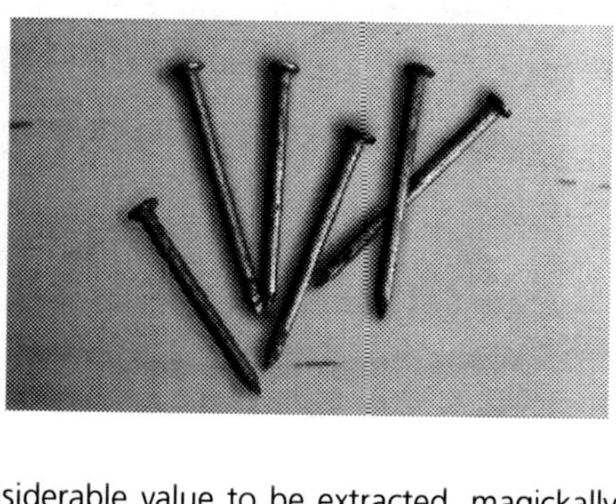

There is also considerable value to be extracted, magickally-speaking, in 'found objects': various things that the universe decides to present you with on your travels.

These may include (but may not be limited to) peculiar stones and sticks found out while walking in the wilds, stray scraps of newspaper or other printed papers which might blow into your face (pay extreme attention to the words on the pages!), animal bones or horns, foreign coins[1], 'road litter' (including roadkill, pieces smashed off from vehicles, which lie in the gutter etc) and feathers. Anything you "accidentally find" may indeed be a manifestation of the universe's desire for you to use them magickally, so get into the habit of carrying a rolled-up bag (or have deep pockets in a favourite coat) to ease the collection of such items....

Once we had to employ a very large rucksack to slowly struggle home with a particularly huge piece of quartz, some 40 pounds in weight, which suddenly fell (literally) 'at our feet' when out walking in some deliciously craggy and remote Welsh hills.

Since it failed to kill us (when by plain geometry and the timing of its 'random' fall it should have splashed our brains over a considerable area of ground, precluding many subsequent adventures in the process) we decided that it would make a useful magical tool for protection. It does.

As does the antler wand illustrated, which has been used from the moment it was acquired, again during a walk in the wilds, with no ritual consecration required, to great effect.

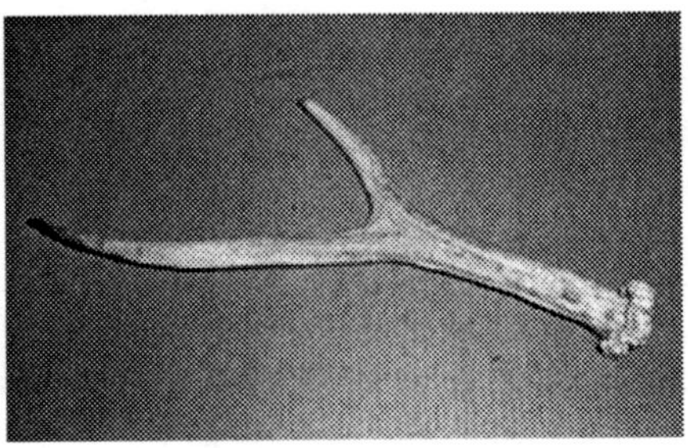

As partially covered above, since many of the techniques in here could be best described as morally ambivalent, there was originally going to be a

1 Since the recent introduction of the standardised Euro currency into many European countries, replacing many other different kinds of money, the variety of unusual foreign coinage to be found has reduced, making such occurrences now much more interesting when they do actually occur.

long section here about magical ethics, which may have been useful for the reader to digest first, or not, depending on whether such matters bother you.

But we decided that anyone who works magick should already have Hir[2] own broad-brush but fluid general standards based on their own experiences, without our waffle to muddy the waters (or not be read at all), so we chose to keep the ethics matters very brief (and ambivalent, and at the end of the book in any case, where few may bother to venture) and add more useful here instead of foisting reams of heavy moral philosophy on you. Thus your acts with this material, and the results, are your own responsibility. Your own moral code for your life today is best in any case, as has been the stumbling block of many an organised religion with numerous inbuilt 'thou shalt nots', which tend to become very dated after a millennia or two. Although saying that, we have just noticed how lovely an Ox you have, and we would really rather like it....

Some of the contents herein have already been printed elsewhere in some abbreviated form (usually in small-circulation 'pagan' magazine articles in the UK), or on the glowing, growing global consciousness that is the internet, but most of it has not, prior to printing here. Where anything has already appeared before then those articles have been expanded on or improved in some way here - we don't do tired rehashes purely for profit.

2 She and Hir are non gender-specific personal pronouns, which we think come from the late great Dr Timothy Leary (RIP). If not his invention then he used them a lot in his writings.

Hunting High and Low

So, cunning craft.... To a large extent the magick here is 'low', i.e. sorcery, in much the same way that the 'cunning folk', the tinkers, folk healers and everyday wart charmers of earlier centuries plied their trade (for which see several excellent books by a British academic Dr Owen Davies, and others for a historical take on the subject).

This work here is not about conjuring the Holy Guardian Angel, we are here doing things to 'make things happen', on earth, and for practical, not spiritual purposes. In earlier times this would be works like magically curing your chickens of failing to lay any eggs and thus starving your family, which on an immediate level in mediaeval times was considerably more important, 'day-to-day' and pragmatic than intellectual contact with higher intelligences and the resulting spiritual advancement would ever have been. Both elements of magick have their time and place, of course. One of the qualities of a really good magickian is knowing when to work in which sphere.

The cunning man or woman of old would have travelled around the locale performing their craft with probably a bag full of herbs, some pins, a flint and tinder to make fire, some ready-made charms, a knife and a weighty book or two (about anything) with which to impress the illiterate.

One of the seeds of this book was a discussion with a friend about what a modern cunner would carry around with them, by comparison. The 21st Century chaos cunner is likely to have a groovy backpack to carry various problem-solving tools in, like a cellphone, a cigarette lighter, a swiss army knife[3], a packet of Ibuprofen[4], a bag of a quite different herbs for ingestion in various ways, some pagan 'bling'[5], a copy of Norton Utilities for the

3 Probably a trade-mark icon is needed here, but you probably know the kind of thing we mean, one of those neat 'boys toys' with about 25 blades and attachments that fits into a very small space, only about three of the blades of which will ever be used for their designed purpose, and some will never be used at all for anything other than cleaning out your fingernails or cutting off plastic packaging from shop-bought items.

4 A common painkiller and anti-inflammatory medical drug.

5 A term shamelessly stolen from the Rap scene; meaning 'over-the-top jewellery', of the kind often displayed by those for whom wearing a velvet cloak should be made a capital offence. As our dear friend Kate Hoolu always says, 'the only good use for velvet is to clean the blood from knives before it clots'.

Computer plus some dark-looking sorcerous books/magazines and probably some weird and discordant sounds on their iPod[6] of the latest hot thing by some cult-famous acid-fried neo-pagan musicians, with which to impress the musically illiterate....

Quite WHAT the modern Chaos Cunner uses to make magic is also a moot point. For example to activate a banishing or malefic spell written on paper one could pin the paper on a Blackthorn spine, which you have ceremonially picked under the baleful glare of a full moon synchronised precisely to the chill midnight chimes of a clock in a deserted, damp, misty churchyard, having first made a solemn offering of one's own blood, some salt, rough bread and ale to the base of the tree, when Jupiter is in Sagittarius and Mercury is retrograde, and casting the spell while reciting an (apparently) traditional rhyme **"wither away, wither away, fade like a shadow at sunset, thou arte under power of mine, wither away, wither away, wither away"** (repeated nine times, with intent, while facing towards the geographical direction of the target of the spell).

Or one could use a shop-bought wooden cocktail stick randomly picked from the packet, at ten minutes past eight on a wet Thursday evening, while waiting for the kettle to boil during an advertisement break between programmes on TV. If the intent is the same, then so is the effect... unless one has a client to impress as well, in which case go for the full-on 'Churchyard Dark Magick Ritual Theatre' option, as it means you can also justify charging more money for the spell (working after 6pm being "double time" for sure), if you are doing some magic for another, on a contract basis.

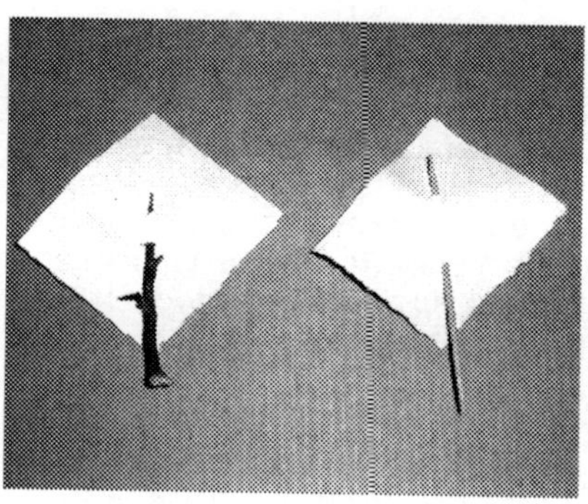

6 Another trademark - a small portable music storage and playback device.

Equally, we have found splendidly and equally useful magical results in dealing with works of 'repelling idiots' when using a wand made from Chinese military bronze crossbow bolt recovered from a battlefield that was approximately 300BC, or a nylon and steel bolt made in 2006. Intent, intent, intent....

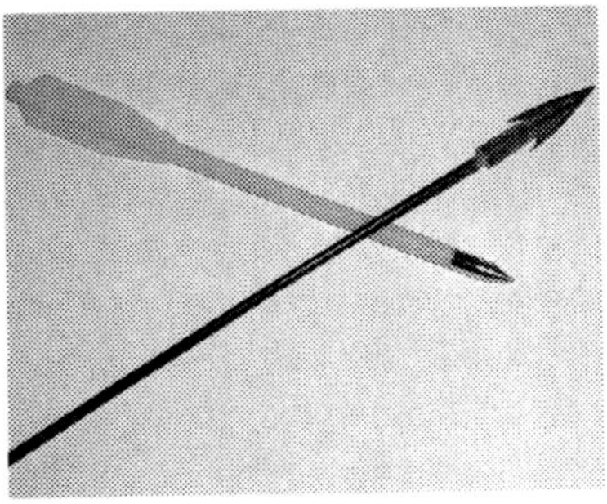

Regardless of what's in the respective Cunner's bag, the kind of problems needing solutions by the Cunner in these times have apparently moved on superficially 'in name' only over the centuries; but not so much as you might think in terms of topic, or indeed in complexity.

Many of the problems afflicting humankind still revolve around the very basics of social interaction, and the terminology is still that of money, power, sex, love, food, health and suchlike, regardless of how it may be buried sometimes under a flurry of new-age or Yuppie-speak obscurities.

Handy Hint:

Whenever confronted by a client with a problem requiring magic, break it down into the most simple summary- is it a spell about love, sex, money, power, revenge or what? There may be combinations of factors, such as revenge on a business rival plus recovery of money from them, or misdirected sexual favours linked to money. This makes it much easier to work out what to do, and it helps in making up your bill at the end; since more complexity means a higher fee....

By the way, the rhyme given above is indeed a totally functional variant of something really rather old. Although we are not claiming any of this book to be hoary 'ye olde magickal traditiones' carried down through the ages and previously rather jealously guarded as secrets by arcane (and-or insane) individuals, traditional magical groups and-or the continuing generations of certain secretive magickal families, *some if it just might be.*

If we were in any way oathbound not to tell the truth about that aspect then we would have to lie about our sources, or we might just be lying about the whole thing. Would it matter in the greater scheme of things, so long as it works?

No.

Times change, but the magic still works in any case. We are often most amused by the antics and impostures of some who claim a hereditary or similar magickal tradition of long lineage, since often those claims take up so much time in their trumpeting that a lot of time is eaten up and not much magic actually seems to be worked.

This is how we do it

Herein we use a few technical terms, of necessity, which should perhaps be explained. One of these is *Gnosis*. This term has become very popular in, if not been totally hijacked by, the Chaos Magick movement, but the origins and practices used to achieve the state indicated by the word predate modern chaos magick by many centuries, and the effects are not exclusively the territory nor property of chaos magicians.

In brief, and in the way meant here, gnosis is a state of being or mind where magick is made easier to happen, and can be like a trance, or an unusual, 'other' mental state. It is the fuel that powers the magick, if you like.

There is also a considerable emotional baggage attached to the word, in that it implies some connection with one or more deities. Also the historical Gnostics were not chaos magicians, which give another conceptual obstacle to clear definition. This deity-connection while doing magick is not always the case, and is not a part of the belief systems of many a mage who follows the 'no-Gods' path, so perhaps gnosis should better be called 'a willed manifestation of a supercharged potential of directed consciousness'.

But that is far clumsier to type, very long-winded to use in conversation, and also carries its' own problems of interpretation, especially the hefty philosophy that underpins trying to explain consciousness, will and manifestation. Even the acronym, 'WMSPDC' is very clumsy, sounding more like the name of some corporate body than anything else. To carry this discussion further would result in an ever-expanding definition, with infinite regress of explanations filling many books and all of that would delay actually doing any damn magick. So we'll call it gnosis for now, with those reservations, and we'll probably call it something else towards the end of the book, once you've done some of the work described herein.

Once you've "been there" you don't need the word anyhow, *it just is*, and like the first orgasm, you will always remember what it feels like.

Imagine the task of trying to explain the concept of heat to a being from another world who had never experienced it, perhaps a being born in the frozen wastes of some far-distant planet, and arriving here in a refrigerated space suit to maintain their own life-form needs of a temperature of below zero. We could talk to them all day of sense organs in our skin, the physics of temperature, draw graphs, show pictures etc, but simply placing their hand in a bowl of pretty warm water for five seconds would circumvent all of that!

It may also kill them, but as we are regularly reminded by paranoid Hollywood science-fiction films often starring fundamentalists of some kind, most aliens are malign and wish us ill, so they deserve it.

So if you think you don't know what gnosis means, we can only suggest that you try to experience it, instead of reading about what it might be like. So enough about what it IS, how do we get there?

Gnosis can be reached in a variety of ways, some of them involuntary, but the proficient Chaos Cunner needs to be able to master several different volitional methods in order to be effective with Hir sorcery. There follows a list of ways to attain Gnosis, which should be indicative, and not considered comprehensive in any way. Devise some methods of your own too!

Ways to attain Gnosis:

- Meditation - learn it from a good book or do a yoga-meditation class in your local area (you don't need to renounce all material possessions, hitch-hike to India and find a Guru to get the basics working for you). Practice!
- Dancing until you either go into trance, or drop to the floor. Then get up and do it again. The waves of free energy generated by the masses, and available in dance clubs and at raves and similar events like music festivals is simply marvellous for this.
- Exhaustion from physical activity ...learning a martial art or two is particularly good for this, as it also teaches various forms of self-discipline, pain control etc, and makes you no soft touch should any idiot think you are a suitable target for mugging... as has been said, why bother going to the trouble of concocting

a complex curse when it is often much easier to simply break someone's face?

- Sex (exhaustion from sex is even better).
- Drugs (but buyer beware!)- this can include excess of legal highs such as extremes of coffee, alcohol, a really very hot spicy chilli or curry meal or the overload of pseudo-endorphins that a truly gluttonous chocolate binge can provide, as well as the common understanding of what taking drugs might actually mean.
- Excess of food of any kind.
- Listening to REALLY loud music for a long time.
- Breathing exercises, including suppression of breath.
- Maintaining a strenuous yogic posture, holding up a heavy weight for a protracted period or some form of uncomfortable restraint.
- Fear: - for example in challenging your own personal fear(s): if you are afraid of heights, doing an abseil or parachute jump for charity can be an awesome means to attain gnosis, as can public speaking for the very shy, or handling a spider if you are mortally afraid of them.
- Pain (this can include body piercing, tattooing, fighting, either for real or in a 'full-on' Martial Arts contact setting, other contact sports, extremes of exercise or a very 'rough' physical session of sex).
- Delight of any kind (this of course may occur in some other categories on this list).
- Mantra or chanting (repetition of seemingly meaningless words or phrases until the mind is 'switched off' from normal consciousness).
- Sacrifice of some kind (be that blood- preferably your own… food, drink or money- try ritually burning a middle-denomination currency note in deliberate fashion and with magical intent to see what gets your gnostic juices flowing… and no cheating; it must be current legal tender in your country, and be your own money, and a sum which you need- if you are very rich the almost meaningless act of burning a mere five-note would achieve little).
- Some 'extraordinary' feat such as fire-walking.
- Visual disturbance, such as from viewing a 'psychedelic' light show or strobes at a rock concert…some personal computer

animation programmes and proprietary 'mind machines' also produce a similar effect, as does laying on you back under a tree in sunlight using the effect of the wind in the leaves to make your visual field flicker.

- Violence and destruction- take a hefty lump of wood or a hammer and break stuff.
- Anger.
- Grief.
- Various diseases that produce fever and-or delirium.
- Vomiting (try quickly swallowing a spoonful or three of vinegar mixed with mustard, lemon juice and horseradish; chased down with a carbonated drink like coca cola or lemonade and then doing some strenuous exercise, 'starjumps' for example).
- Sneezing (try some snuff or freshly ground pepper, with intent).
- Eating a food which you despise, or something 'disgusting' to you, for example Jellied Eels is a personal un-favourite of ours, and 'gets us there' every time!
- Mild electric shock.

That should be plenty to be going on with. Some methods can be combined- such as a chocolate binge followed by inducing vomiting, or sexual activity with restraint and-or electrical play. Use your own ingenuity.

As the late and rather marvellous Dr Hunter S Thompson once wrote: **"I hate to advocate drugs, alcohol, violence, or insanity to anyone... but they've always worked for me"**.

Obviously some of the above methods, such as drugs, breath suppression and electric shocks are medically dangerous and for legal reasons we must also say that they are most unwise to employ, but were included here to give a more comprehensive overview of the various keys to gnosis that have been used through the ages, so this is history, not incitement, OK?

Research all intended methods for their pros and cons before you try anything, and bear in mind that gnosis carried too far, like anything, can harm and-or kill you if handled clumsily.

Handy Hint:

Having a severe delirious disease could of course be fatal, and might affect the concentration needed to make magick, but when you have the 'flu or a bad cold, don't just lay there bemoaning your illness, give a few spells a try, you may be pleasantly surprised by the results. We were- some of the more interesting, meaningful and effective variations of technique presented in this book arose when we had the 'flu.

The other main topic to be defined is Sigils. These are one of the famous derivations from the English sorcerer, philosopher and artist Austin Osman Spare, whose life and achievements have been already covered to great depth by such writers as Kenneth Grant, Ramsey Dukes, Gavin Semple and others.

Okay, so what is a sigil? It is a practical, visual means to encode a spell, so that it becomes a powerful symbol. If you merely write an intent on a piece of paper in English it *may* work, if you give it heaps of gnostic propulsion. If that intent is sigilised, for some reason it becomes much easier (and 'cheaper' in terms of the amount of gnostic 'oomph' required) to make it work. Don't ask us how, it just happens that way.

We could write for hours about sigils, but in the scope of this small book we must be brief, and just show you a few examples of how to make them. There are other methods available out there, find those that work best for you....

Like any successful magic, it all starts with an intent. Let's pick something simple for the sake of illustration. Imagine you have an important examination or test coming up. You will of course be revising and doing all the academic things needed of you, but to add a magical impetus you may want to prepare a sigil to help you if for example you have had previous anxiety problems in exam situations. So you intent might reasonably be that when you enter the exam room you will be calm and collected. If your problem is remembering things in a certain relevant order then you may focus on boosting your powers of recall. There are plenty of other things that you could give a magical boost to.

Whatever it is needs to be phrased in the form of a concise magical intent, perhaps like this:

It is my Will that in my Examination I will be Totally Calm

Now it needs to be visually encoded, and the first step is to remove any duplicate letters, so that leaves you with:

I t s m y W l h a n E x o b c

Now we turn the letters into a drawn symbol, which can be graphically re-arranged in any number of ways (including stretching letters, and re-using parts of one to include another, such as the lines of the T also being the lines that form an upside-down L) to form a pictorial device that uses all of those letters as constituent shapes, perhaps like this below (only a suggestion) which contains all the letters given above, but in a form that is not recognisable to the literate-analytical mind:

As you can see, it does not require fabulous drawing skills, but if you are able to add some flourishes and design factors to your sigils that obscure the textual basis even more, then please do.

If you can in any way arrange the letters into a shape that visually implies the intent in some way, then all the better. For example we have on occasions prepared sigils for safe and prompt airline flights that resemble a plane, or a bird in flight, and some 'defensive' sigils for a house, that actually looked very like the battlements of a mediaeval castle.

Charge the sigil, using one or more means of gnosis as discussed above, *then put the sigil away in a safe place and forget about it*. It may be useful to have a particular safe place to keep all your sigils, like a metal box or some arcane-looking chest. If you are preparing a number of sigils for many purposes over time, you will actually forget which weird drawing means what, so it is advisable, if this is relevant, to add a date to the rear of the paper on which date the sigil can be burned, having 'expired' and being no longer needed (for example this would be a date some brief while after your last exam, in the example given above). Some sigils may be much longer term in scope, or perhaps even lifetime-duration based, in which case indicate that on the back of the paper.

In fact for such very longterm sigils it may be advisable to inscribe or engrave them on metal, wood, glass or stone, perhaps draw them in wet cement, mould them in clay, or paint them onto something with a little more permanence and longevity than paper. Once you have drawn up your sigil for any purpose, destroy (preferably burn) any draft papers used for 'working out' the design etc, so that all that remains is the final version of the spell.

To a large extent the scope of using sigils is only limited by the cunner's ingenuity in finding new ways to prepare them, and new ways to use them, it is a quite superb and rapid means to cast an effective spell.

One method we find useful when communicating with people by email, and if we wish to pass on any desire to them, is to prepare an email message that has each sentence starting with a succeeding letter from our abbreviated sigil-phrase for that desire. We have also done it with some passages of this book, (and you cannot tell, can you?) and some of our other writings.

An older-tech method, from when people use to use faxes a lot, was to draw a small sigil on the edge of the paper to be faxed, then to blot the ink so that the sigil was not recognisable as such.... Fax transmissions used to be so poor in visual quality that one more blotch on the margin was not going to be noticed, but the sigil would be received for sure.

Equally, there is such ease in having t-shirts printed nowadays that you can incorporate a sigil in a design and literally wear your desire on your chest, for all to see and none to understand.

As an aside, having a really very important sigil permanently tattooed onto your body (perhaps within an artistic design as well) is a fabulous way to set the sigil working, as the minor but prolonged pain of being tattooed (and the bloodletting involved) can be used to achieve a gnosis that can be internally – and eternally, so long as blood flows in your veins - recycled to 'fire the sigil off'.

This book is not the place for discussing it, but Spare's method of Sigils is but a tiny offshoot of his work, and perhaps nowhere near the most important part of it, in much the same way as saying that some bloke called Orson Welles once did a rather good radio show about aliens, and then not delving any further into his remarkable career in the arts. The philosophy and art underlying Spare's work is worth a lot of your time; so go find out some more.

Sudoku and Magic Squares

An additional way to sigilise desires is to use a magical square. In past times these squares were prescriptive, coming from old sorcery books like the Key of Solomon, and were usually aligned to planetary magic. For example there were squares to the Sun, Moon, Mercury etc, which were used to draw magical symbols related to the spiritual intelligences of those planets, and used for spells of those nature, for example Mercury in works of communication.

Nowadays there is a potential new magic square to be found in your daily newspaper (or books, or on the internet), in the popular new puzzle game know as Sudoku (which no doubt is also a registered trademark), which uses many permutations of number grids. It is a good logical-process/ mental exercise in any case, but doing a sudoku puzzle *creates* your own magic square, such as this:

2	5	8
9	1	3
7	4	6

and the concentration involved in getting the puzzle right is a means of approaching pre-gnosis. Then one creates a desire to be sigilised as before, and this may for example produce the unique letters:

ITSMYWLGAEPCR

Using their alphabetical position to assign a number (A=1, B=2 etc) these letters can be converted to numbers as follows:

A =1	B=2	C=3	D=4	E=5	F=6
G=7	H=8	I=9	J=10 (1)	K=11 (2)	L=12 (3)
M=13 (4)	N=14 (5)	O=15 (6)	P=16 (7)	Q=17 (8)	R=18 (9)
S=19 (1)	T=20 (2)	U=21 (3)	V=22 (4)	W=23 (5)	X=24 (6)
Y=25 (7)	Z=26 (8)				

Any letter with a double-digit number is adapted to a single digit by adding the two numbers, for examples: L, being 12 becomes 1=2 =3 and S, being 19 which then becomes 10, which becomes 1 (which is indicated in brackets in the table above).

Thus the above example of ITSMYWLGAEPCR
becomes translated to 9 2 1 4 7 6 3 7 1 5 7 3 9

Taking a piece of tracing paper and placing it over the sudoku magic square you have created, use these numbers on the square as coordinates to draw out a sequential pattern of the sigil numbers, as you go from the first number to the second, to the third etc., like this:

Which becomes a completely- and uniquely- encoded sigil for the desire. Since the sudoku grids are open to huge variance the chances against ever making two identical sigils for the same desire are phenomenal. Charge the sigil *via* whatever method of gnosis suits, and put it away somewhere safe as before.

There is also no reason why the simple A=1, B=2 example encoding method should be used exclusively, a reverse system where A=26, B=25 or any other variation on that can be used, and the chaos cunner who is intent on doing a lot of these workings would do well to make up a series of many different alphabet grids with various different numerical assignments made, and perhaps choose one at random to be the key-code for that day's (or hour's) sigilising work. Alternatively, the more complex sudoku puzzles using grids of more than nine numbers allow for a completely different pattern and alpha-numeric encoding system to be used entirely.

If you wish to really be intense about it, an embroidered sigil can be hugely effective, especially if you embroider it onto an item of clothing, in a place where it is not visible, and wear that item for as long as the sigil is needed to be active. In the process of embroidery you are very likely to feed the sigil a little gnosis with blood from needle-pricks, which helps.

Rituals to Prevent Pursuit

This is a pretty basic need for many. Imagine that someone is chasing you. Or some*thing*....

Damn scary, isn't it? Have you ever had dreams like that?

Yeah, us too.... It happens in waking consciousness too.

First you need to know that 'fear is failure', and the fear of being caught is what needs to be addressed magickally. Once that little philosophical nugget is spoken out loud and shoulders are shrugged, what do you do next? It doesn't help much, does it? What do you do to stop the pursuit, whether it be in 'real life' or 'dream' states?

In an ideal world you would be able to turn around, hold up your hand and simply ask the pursuer to just stop, and they would do so, being a reasonable human being. Since we do not live in an ideal world, and people can be utter wankers, sometimes a magical intervention is needed. Or you can biff them on the nose sufficiently hard to break bones, and loudly tell them to fuck off, as you see fit; whichever is the quicker and easier option. Don't jump straight to the two-hour ritual magical solution if it can be dealt with in one minute by physical means.

The meaning of 'chased' is also open to much and wide interpretation; we suggest that this work would function equally well for repelling persistent or nuisance stalkers as for deflecting an over-zealous Tax Office (IRS for American readers). It will also serve to protect against magickal attack, on the really very few occasions that the latter thing ever actually happens and is not simple paranoia... or even being a complex paranoia which has derived from taking far too many drugs. Or in some few cases (we know who you are, and so do you...) from not taking *enough* of the drugs you are supposed to.

"Way back when..." date unknown, in much the same way that 'Ancient Briton' or 'Original Celtic' seems so meaningful but actually means nothing, being an explanatory fiction so far as historians are concerned...

"in the mists of time"... someone (also unknown) invented this beastie (see picture below), a piece of heavy fabricated iron with sharpened points, used to prevent their pursuit by horses.

The idea was, you had a bag-ful of them, and scattered them off the back of your horse (or from your horse-drawn cart) onto the track behind you when being pursued, and due to the shape and configuration of the arms, each one always lands on the ground, braced, with one point uppermost. It's a nifty precursor to the modern warfare technique of mine-laying, we guess. You can perhaps imagine how these things would stop pursuing cavalry dead in their tracks (literally) once a full-speed hoof landed on them.

Pause here to wince.

The coin in the bottom of the picture is there to give some perspective, it's a UK One Pence piece, being around 2cm in diameter.

A version of this item, using bent iron nails welded together in the same functional tetrahedral shape was also used to some great effect during the Miners' Strike in the UK in the 1980s, to stop Police Cars, mostly, as they will kill rubber pneumatic tyres on a tarmac road just as well as they would penetrate animal hooves on a forest track.

It is interesting to note as an aside that the tetrahedral structure is basically the same shape as the Carbon atom, the source of all life as we know it, and the miners were of course digging up coal, a different form of Carbon, but one with huge survival value... now there's a possibly unconscious job-protection sigil! A shame it didn't work, ultimately, so far as looking at the numbers of coal miners now employed in the UK, compared to back then.

Modern police forces in many countries use an articulated bar based on this kind of thing, called a 'stinger' to throw across a road to rapidly stop the cars of criminals which are being pursued. We got our version of this piece of kit second-hand (but from a source that was very much 'old-school sorcery' in style and moral outlook), so we have no idea what it was made for. We suspect from the design and rough but competent workmanship that it is at least few decades old - it is not pretty, but most functional. And from the 'feel', it *has* been used. And for magickal purposes, ours WORKS.

This is a 'make something' piece of magic, so it needs access to tools and materials. If you are one of the few who have a welding kit and the requisite skills, then make the 'traditional' version; using four nails or sharpened iron rods.

However, assuming you are in the majority of likely readers of this book who do not have a welding workshop immediately to hand there is an alternative way to make something that will do the same job, magickally speaking.

You will need four very long and sharp nails (six inch nails, or the metric equivalent), a hockey or cricket ball (or a baseball for those in the USA) or some kind of very solid hardwood sphere of roughly the same size (4-5 inches diameter), a very sharp knife, a hammer, a power drill, with a drill bit a fraction thinner than the diameter of the shaft of the nails, a rough file, a hacksaw (or bolt cutters) and some epoxy resin glue.

An engineering vice will also be very useful to help prevent too much bloodshed. If you have goggles, then wear them, since as well as protecting your eyes it gives the manufacturing proceedings an air of the 'mad scientist at work', which always helps the imagery and general atmosphere in works of results magick like this. If you have an 'Einstein'-type wig or white lab coat (for any reason at all), or something of that nature to give a semblance of 'mad scientist', then wear that too, while ensuring that nothing of your costume becomes caught in the drill while you are using it. If you already have long hair, back-comb it for the duration of the manufacturing process.

Spray paint is optional, and your manic laughter while playing very loud 'doomy' rock music during the manufacture of this item is bordering on the compulsory. A particular favourite soundtrack for this task would be something dark and unpleasant performed by the Sisters of Mercy or Fields of the Nephilim. Ensure you turn up the bass frequencies to distortion levels, as this is not a piece of 'arts and crafts' work, this is simply WAR.

With great care, cut four small nicks in the skin of the ball, in a tetrahedral configuration. You may find a protractor useful for this, or it can, with care, be done "by eye"... you can work out roughly where the holes should be by taking a small piece of some modeling clay, making a ball and pushing matches or cocktail sticks into it until you have the right pattern, and then copying that configuration on the full-size version. Absolutely precise angles to within aeronautical engineering error-tolerances are not necessary, so long as the thing will drop every time with one point uppermost.

Drill out the ball, slowly and carefully, until you have made a hole around an inch deep towards the centre, at the pretty much correct angle, in each site where you made a cut. If the ball is leather-covered rather than a hard plastic or wooden practice ball, then a rather 'charnel' burning flesh smell will be produced by the drilling, which may be effective in emphasising the purpose of the rite to one's senses.

Use boltcutters or a good sharp hacksaw to take the head off each nail, coat the cut end (formerly the head end) with epoxy glue and carefully insert the de-headed end of the nail into the hole in the ball. Tap gently home using the hammer, holding a small block of wood over it to protect the nail point (and your hammer) until it is in the hole firmly.

Carefully repeat with each hole, then leave the object somewhere safe overnight for the glue to completely set. You might wish to create a related sigil to place under your pillow for this night, based on the protective intent of the item you are now making.

You can if you wish spray-paint the ball black or some other colour to suit your mood and-or the exact ritual intent. We have seen one of these things painted in festive silver, gold and metallic green spirals, and most prettily dressed up with tinsel and baubles at Christmas time, when simultaneously being most successfully used to magickally prevent unwanted relatives ever visiting again.

Delicious.

Be sure to carefully file the points of the nails until they are really very sharp indeed. You might also want to buy a 'carborundum' sharpening stone from a hardware or tool shop, to give the filed edges a really finely-honed point, bordering on surgical sharpness. Take time and pride in doing this just right. The rhythmic grating sound and repetitive movement involved can also be used to attain a mild meditative gnosis, as can the hacksawing of the nails, done previously - it's a workshop sound mantra if you like. From now on handle this item with great care, as it will WANT to make you bleed.

The activation ritual is quite simple, perform a banishing ritual as you will (or not) and then, choosing your own means of gnosis, name your pursuer(s) out loud, name the intent of the spiked ball (to prevent their pursuit), and throw the spiked ball behind you, visualising their pursuit of you coming to a very rapid, catastrophic and sticky end as they encounter the 'real world' analogues of what the ball represents. Choose the visualisation wisely, as well as the choice of exactly where you throw the thing… inadvertently sticking it in the wall, your partner, some piece of domestic electrical hardware or a pet is not a great start to working with the object.

When you are content that your visualisation is complete, pick up the spiked ball with a gloved hand and place in a solid container, such as a bucket or metal box (a large biscuit/cookie tin perhaps), and cover it with a solid lid and put it somewhere away safe away from prying eyes and careless hands, until such time as it may be needed again.

In a similar vein, you may also be interested in the *Nightmare Catcher Rite*, which is to be found further along in the book.

For legal reasons we should here remark that this is a **purely symbolic piece of magick**. *To literally throw such an item into the path of someone or some animal (or a vehicle) will probably entail you making all manner of court attendances and-or getting a reputation for being a cruel, twisted bastard, who is then under future suspicion by the police whenever anything nasty happens locally, which is rather counter-productive to the intent of the ritual, to free you of accretions.*

The item can also be used for divination; of the kind where the answer has a quaternary split, for example a question that could have answers of "yes, for sure", "probably yes", "probably not" and "no way", would suit this beautifully - paint a small letter, number, coloured spot or symbol (of your own choosing) on each spike, to indicate one answer from the above four permutations, then ask the question seriously and toss the thing high up in the air behind you, ensuring that it spins rapidly while falling.

Avoid getting in the way of the thing as it comes crashing back to earth. The spine that sticks uppermost carries the answer to your question, unless one spine sticks firmly into the ground (or floor) in which case take that answer!

There is some more about divination methods later in the book.

It will have occurred to some, while reading the above construction plans, that by employing some simple geometry and using 4 more nails, a nice spiky 8-pointed chaos-star ball can be made. If it occurred to you, then do it! Once made, work out some ritual uses for the thing, using your own ingenuity.

If the Shoe fits...

A simpler (in that there is no 'Workshop 101' element), faster and incredibly effective rite to use if you actually know who is doing the pursuit is this:

If you are able to get access to the person's home by whatever means, steal one of their shoes (or, failing that, socks, stockings or tights- the latter being 'pantyhose' to US readers, depending on their gender and-or dress sense). This could be done while innocently visiting their bathroom and quickly delving into a laundry basket or nipping into a bedroom and speedily rifling the wardrobe while an accomplice distracts the target elsewhere in the house, by admiring their music collection, their garden, their pets, children, or something similarly time-consuming.

Preferably take the 'right foot', as in this 90% right-handed world that is symbolically the 'leading foot', but no matter if not, so long as you get a physical link to your target's means of locomotion. If you suspect this person will be a major problem to you in future, also take the trouble to obtain a small item of clothing for possible use in an 'effigy' piece of image magic (see later in the book).

Purloining a shoe from their hallway might be a bit too suspicious, since something found in that location might indicate a regularly-used item whose absence will be quickly noticed. However footwear kept in wardrobes and drawers tend to be those used less often, perhaps a seasonal item, and equally often they have a habit of becoming innocently separated in the course of normal life, especially if there are young children or mischievous dogs in the house.

Your target's subsequently being unable to find the missing other half of a pair in an untidy wardrobe would not arouse too much suspicion, only annoyance (which emotion arising in them, being distracting, can only help your cause in hindering their pursuit of you).

Remove the item from the house without suspicion or detection, and take it quickly to a place that is a 'dead end' in reality as well as symbolically, be that an actual *cul-de-sac* in a road, or a footpath that ends in a wall, cliff edge or solid fence, or find a very quiet piece of land inside a graveyard, right up against the outer wall[7].

Face the shoe (or sock, or other purloined object) with the toe end towards the wall, and advance it until the toe just touches the barrier, such that it cannot move forward any more. Using a trusty hammer (or the heel of your own shoe), drive one of the large nails mentioned in a Hint Box earlier, that you perhaps now carry with you by habit, through that point of the shoe (or item) where the wearer's 'arch' of their foot would be.

Continue hitting, to drive the nail into the ground. With visualised, ritual intent. And leave the object there, unable to move forward due to the barrier, and unable to move at all due to the nail. Obscuring it with some local vegetation or soil as camouflage would also be advisable, to prevent it being disturbed by local animals or by curious passing humans right away.

7 If you choose a graveyard, take this opportunity to re-stock on your supplies of graveyard dirt, which is a very useful spell ingredient in some circumstances. Simply having visitors to your house see a jar labelled Graveyard Dirt on your magical equipment shelves helps your sorcerous reputation no end, even if it is never used, or indeed if it is simply mundane mud dug up from a secular garden, or horticultural compost purchased from a shop, mixed with a handful of flour, some small sticks and gravel to give an interesting visual consistency. If you are in the graveyard early in the morning grab some dew from the long grass by using a clean handkerchief tied around one ankle too (and afterwards put the kerchief in a clean plastic bag right away), as Graveyard Dew is also a powerful ingredient in spellcasting.

Handy Hint:

Piercing with nails and suchlike is not always a negative act. It is important in your magic to think laterally- the image below is not the malign thing that it might first appear, but in fact a rite for fertility, for a couple who were having conception problems. The symbolism of removing blocks should be obvious, the thorn piercing the condom is LITERALLY 'a prick', which "gets through". For US readers the trademark may not be familiar, think 'Trojan'. At the time of writing the child that resulted is just about learning to talk....

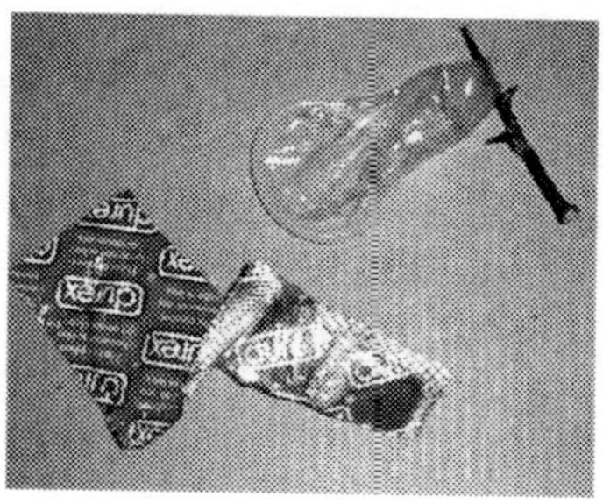

A Blow Job: Wind, Magic and Chaos

There is a long association with magicians working with the natural environment, including the weather. This section deals very briefly with some manifestations of the Wind, and concludes with a practical method of working with modern windmills.

The North Berwick witches were executed nearly 400 years ago for allegedly raising a storm to sink King James' ship. He survived, and tried them *personally,* (can you imagine THAT happening today? Jeez, what an effect that must have had on society…!) which brought the idea of wind, witchcraft and such things very much into the public eye….

Hastur is a wind demon in the fiction associated with HP Lovecraft, that writer so beloved of many a chaos magician and role-playing gamer. It seems that Hastur was actually a name borrowed from earlier authors, and a word that Lovecraft used only briefly. The 'Hastur who is the Wind Walker' is actually an invention of the author August Derleth, Lovecraft's friend, literary executor and successor in the genre… but anyway… the very interesting magician Stephen Sennitt wrote of some extreme Chaos magickal work with Hastur, which was characterised by "a black titan windstorm… with a merciless frenzy", this being at the same date as 'the great storm' the most recent UK hurricane in October 1987, with force 12 winds and a freakily unseasonable, and scientifically most remarkable six degree rise in temperature in a few hours. Given their more regular and media-covered weather-related disasters, US readers may not be especially impressed by this, but for Britain this was an incredible, once in 250-year storm, and it has had a profound and continuing effect on the landscape, both physical and mental.

This storm brought overnight devastation to the southern half of England and Wales, and Northern France. Over fifteen million trees were blown down and substantial damage was caused to buildings, cars and shipping, with hundreds of roads and railway lines blocked by debris. The mercifully small number of 18 people died, perhaps because the full force of the storm hit the land in the small hours, when the majority of people would have been indoors and asleep.

The 'Hay' *Necronomicon*, a modern print version of that alleged dread book describes the voice of Hastur as "the mournful sigh of the vortex, the mad rushing of the Ultimate Wind that Swirls darkly among the silent stars... whose ceaseless roaring ever fills the timeless skies.... His might teareth the forest and crusheth the city..." Yup, sounds about right to us... which is odd, as the 'Hay' *Necronomicon* (as are all others, most likely) a fake... allegedly.

The 'psychic quester' Andrew Collins gives the same date as Sennitt for some very weird things happening, but these were, in Collins' perception major 'black magical workings' being afoot in Southern Britain. Psychic questing is a recent development in occult and New Age circles, being started around 1979 by Collins and his associates. Also known simply as 'questing', with a terminology and slang all of its own, Collins describes it as a technique whereby psychic individuals are taken out of the confines of indoor séances and living-room divinations, and employed 'on-site' in the external world.

First-hand psychic impressions of ancient, sacred sites and churchyards are used by Collins and other researchers to detect hidden (usually buried) objects, be they archaeological finds or more recent esoteric articles ritually placed in the ground by living individuals, for magical purposes.

These individuals are often involved in 'Black Magic', according to Collins, whose 'White' occult group is opposed to them. The location and retrieval of physical objects gives some veracity to the psychic impressions, but there will always be the suspicion of trickery somewhere along the line, and that's outside the scope of this piece...

We rather like and enjoy what he writes, for what it's worth, but with a large pinch of salt always to hand. Collins' several books on this theme are described as 'non-fiction' but are written in a racy, 'thriller' style, with characters that are often composites of several individuals who had more minor roles in the alleged actual events. As such, his writings often come across to the reader as exciting, escapist novels.

Collins himself admits that this may all sound like a Dennis Wheatley or Tolkien story at times, and we've not yet had a chance to read one of his latest tomes, where it seems that the disembodied shade of Aleister Crowley led him to find the Holy Grail.

Heck, nothing that interesting ever seems to happen around these parts....

Collins reports several of 'his' psychics having terrifying visions of dark wolves just prior to, and on the night of the 1987 great storm, and this can be easily paralleled to various early modern visions of 'greate evil dogges' associated with mighty storms. The story of the Wizard of Oz has a helluva wind, too... are people hitting on some archetype here, d'you think?

The 1987 storm in the UK followed much the same course and hit the same area of the last truly huge storm to hit Southern Britain, in November 1703. That storm, coming without any forewarning *via* the benefit of modern weather-tracking satellite equipment (and Television news to spread the word) was a total surprise and caused massive damage. Over a hundred were killed on land, and the entire village and church of Kingston Gorse in Sussex was literally flattened. We suspect that this site, being thus very charged with that 'elemental force' would be a rather good place to do some elemental magic of Air, such as the rite discussed below.

Four hundred wooden windmills were destroyed across the country - some of them being spun so fast by the wind that they caught FIRE from the resultant friction, much like a 'Catherine Wheel' firework. This must have appeared particularly demonic to horrified observers, and probably impossible to imagine for us, all cosy and secure in the 21st Century. It may be coincidence or a desire to create correspondences, but the magical sigil for Hastur, which Stephen Sennit gives in his grimoire[8] bears a striking resemblance to a simple sketch of a windmill.

At sea the British fleet was decimated, losing hundreds of ships and over 8,000 sailors, with additional heavy merchant shipping losses.

The Eddystone Lighthouse, a vital aid to shipping, was also destroyed in the storm. The loss of so many sailors was a serious threat to national security, and

8 The formerly rare book Liber Koth, which we understand has recently had a much-deserved reprint, so it should be easier to find nowadays.

the damage to windmills and heavy flooding, which drowned many thousands of food animals and tainted crop fields (from the massive ingress of salt water into the soil from the storm-driven extra-high tide) was a major threat to regional food stocks for some time to come, with consequent likely loss of life, as an official report of the time said: **"Tis thought most of their land will be worth but little this 2 or 3 years"**... This gives a very slight idea of what those poor folk all over Asia must have experienced with the Tsunami of late 2004.

In times of efficient international food supply infrastructure and supermarkets in every town, the storm of 1987 was considerably less of a threat so far as day-to-day nutrition was concerned - a few folk had to live on cold tinned food for a while until they got their power lines re-connected, that was about all. Nobody was in any real danger of starving to death last time around. However the 1987 event still managed to scare a great many people, and changed the landscape for decades to come. Many of the long-distance country views opened up by the absence of trees had not been visible for 250 years, literally changing people's consciousness overnight, so far as what they could actually SEE.

We remember being outside in the early stages of the storm, hearing the nightmarish screaming of the wind in overhead cables (the Aeolian Harp effect) and thinking that this could well be a night to remember. Much whooping went on later when a series of large trees crashed down very near, and we could feel the earth shaking repeatedly as other trees were knocked down as if they were match-sticks. Gnosis from shock and destruction can be useful, but we would rather the effect on the environment in that storm had been far less than it ultimately was.

The influential 20th century magician Kenneth Grant and his Nu-Isis lodge had ritual dealings with Hastur in the 1950s, including an alleged 'indoor hurricane' while all outside was, very spookily, completely still, and in some quarters the Elizabethan court magus Dr John Dee is reputed to have magically raised the storm that saw off the Armada, saving England from invasion and conquest... given all the more credence as it appears that no Spanish ship was actually sunk by naval action, it was all done by the wind. Even today, coastal witches are still successfully 'selling the wind' to becalmed sailors.

Well, that's just a little flavour...what follows is a bit of chaotic wind magic; and we're not calling up demons or raising storms....

It does rather depend on where you live, but several areas of the UK and overseas have modern windfarms - I'm sure you've at least seen a photo of them - huge white space-age metal towers with mighty spinning blades, scattered across the country.

At rest, the two-bladed ones stand like enormous Tau crosses, which is kinda spooky in a crucifixion kind of way when you come to the top of a hill and find them all waiting silently... some pagans hate them, some love them, but we are stuck with the things, and they are at least only a bit noisy, and not liable to go into meltdown and contaminate the land for 250,000 years, like some other sources of power....

It was only during a period in 2002 when we were regularly driving across some windmill-infested countryside that it struck us how magically very useful they might be as a tool. They are effectively 'prayer wheels' on a huge scale, and to add to the potential magical effect, they are linked into the national electricity grid... a magical link is all very well, but the windmills are by definition *physically linked* to every building in the country via the electrical current which they create and send down a copper wire, which goes all the way to the domestic appliances that people plug into their wall sockets.

Copper wire was once a component of 'traditional' magical wands, forming a central core (like the graphite in a pencil) to conduct the magical 'fluence' (for examples see ancient ceremonial magick books like the *Key of Solomon*).

You will also see any number of copper-bound crystal-festooned staffs and wands at New Age fayres.... [9]

So, the copper link gives a lovely, direct and physical means to send a spell to anywhere, or anyone, you wish....

A spontaneous piece of chaos work ensued. A simple sigil to contain the intent of the working was rapidly formulated and prepared for casting. It was decided that as there is so much motion and spiralling force involved in the windmills that a passive form of gnosis - in this case meditation-visualisation of the sigil and how it would travel to the target rapidly, down the humming, pulsing copper power lines - would be better than any active gnosis method such as wild dancing.

Any gnosis-inducing spin generated by humans in dance or exercise would be completely and embarrassingly puny by comparison to the awesome power of the windmills.

At gnosis the sigil was mentally projected onto the spinning blades (and by driving around to the other side of the windmills you can choose a clockwise or anticlockwise spin, to suit your intention - be it creation or negation magic) and that was it.

Highly effective and impressive results followed within a mere 40 minutes and so we offer this as a potential technique for those with a will to experiment. It's also a very interesting example of the kind of improvisational magic that a Chaos Cunner should perpetually try to keep inventing, and this one we call 'Quixotic Chaos', which if we could be bothered we might consider attaching a trademark to.

After some panicked waving and miming of 'death by being sucked up into a vortex and chopped to small pieces by whirling blades', from

9 As an aside, quite why copper is seen to be so 'friendly' to the earth-first new age pagan brigade when copper mining is done with such disregard to the land is beyond us. It's just like all those supposedly 'healing crystals' which result from explosive mining of the ground, tearing at the heart of Gaia- how surprising that none of the supposed psychics ever tune into THAT!... and at great risk to the poor foreign miners who probably get paid 2 dollars a day at best for working underground in hostile and dangerous places, often using hideously poisonous chemicals to separate out minerals from the waste rock, and having a resultant life-expectancy of around 35. So, Heal the Earth - DON'T buy fucking crystals....

someone with legal qualifications we must also mention that it would be extremely dangerous to make a sigil and attempt to physically cast it into the actual spinning blades. You only have to see the appalling gory mess that these windmills occasionally make of large (and presumably myopic) birds like Swans to appreciate that.

These big windmills are too high to physically reach, anyhow, and a lot of them, like in our photograph, are behind fences, so the danger of anyone actually succeeding in substantially casting an actual material sigil into the blades is low, but you know how very stupid some people can be, right?

Love Spells for Fun and Profit

You will, as a chaos cunner, on plenty of occasions be asked to intervene in matters of the heart for your clients. Enough times to quickly become totally sick of it, anyhow.

Aside from the dubious morality of bewitching one half of a 'happy couple' (or not so happy couple, usually, hence the implied need for magickal intervention), it should also be noted that so-called love spells have a habit of really not working too well, probably because there is an element of working in opposition to at least one person's will. Possibly more than one, if the object of the spell already has a partner, and the intent includes the side-effect of splitting them up to make one of those persons available to the affections of another.

You also need to do your research on the case background. In one case we knew of, much effort and money was expended by a man who wished a woman bewitched towards him. None of the many lengthy and increasingly powerful spells cast for this purpose actually worked. She continued to not approach him in a romantic fashion.

It was only later, when he discovered that she was not heterosexual, that the magical problem here became clear. It may have been easy to make him the object of her affection if she had not been gay, but since she was, the spells were simply not being directed in a way that might have had some success. The spellcaster involved took their money and gracefully withdrew; making sarcastic comments along the lines that trying to nail KY Jelly[10] to the ceiling would have been easier.

So, try to avoid doing love spells at all times, but if you feel you have to become involved, make sure you are paid very well, paid in advance, and on a no fee-no spell basis, with no guarantee of success. When faced with a needy and-or paying customer there are numerous ways to keep the customer occupied using feints, and in keeping them occupied it is sometimes the case that in giving them a complex repeated rite to perform you deflect or dilute their incredible neediness.

10 More trademarks. A proprietary brand of liquid sexual lubricant.

This upfront and obvious neediness may be a turn-off for a potential partner in the first instance, and in the process of keeping them busy your feint will actually contribute towards making them more attractive to others in general. Thus the result is tangential (as our dear Kenneth Grant might say), rather than directly due to the magick, but it's still a result, and one for which you can (and should) take a great deal of credit, take all the money, and enhance any reputation you might wish to gain as a 'kick-ass spellcaster'.

Be warned that gaining such reputations are all well and good, but can be a nuisance for one's anonymity and future private magickal practice, if that is something you wish to cultivate.

So there are some awkward and time-consuming things to obtain that you can ask a client to collect prior to your creating a love ritual, which will be written for them to perform under your direction (such as having them collect a symbolic and high number of rose petals by moonlight, perhaps 77, or 777 if you are feeling especially cruel), and these tasks will keep them occupied, and regardless of any romantic success it will also keep your time free-r for a while.

Instruct your client that before performing any form of ritual they must cleanse and purify their body and mind for three days, five days, ten days (as you see fit, and for however long you wish to be less disturbed by them) prior to the ritual by meditating, and-or fasting or only eating an organic vegetarian diet (i.e. something that takes time to prepare, hence they have less time to bother folk with their neediness), and not drinking alcohol or smoking anything. If they are already Vegetarian suggest a Vegan, or fruit-only diet, in whatever case it needs be something different and time-consuming for them to do. If already Vegan then get them fasting for at least 24 hours, and that will keep them busy by making them think about how hungry they are.

Other things to have them do during this fast is to prepare their own writing charcoal, with which to write out their magical desire. Instruct them to take a walk in the woods, with intent, choose a twig, ask the permission of the tree to take it, ceremonially cut it, perhaps after meditating under that tree for an hour (or two, or three) and leaving an offering of food, something they have made from scratch at home specifically for this offering.... Do you get the picture here? And then advise them to take the twig home, strip the bark carefully and slowly, very slowly 'charcoal' the twig over a pink candle (pink for lurvvvvve). That entire procedure should take an entire day and night, as an absolute minimum. And if you are lucky, much longer.

Your client will also need a piece of plain paper, preferably hand-made. Some ethnic and 'hippy' shops sell coloured rice paper in notebook form, this is ideal... tell the client to pick up several of these and to 'tune in' to which one is the right one; this will not only take more of their time, but reinforce the involved nature of the ritual if even the paper has to be perfect, vibe-wise.

Swan feathers are also a very good tool for love spells - impress the client strongly with the notion that swans mate for life ...there is not actually much scientific evidence for this, as we have read a fascinating paper somewhere about the high levels of 'adultery' in the wildfowl kingdom, but keep that out of the discussion... and emphasise that this is not a trivial spell, and that the things required to work the spell will require great and meaningful effort on the client's part to acquire them.

Have them go for a long walk near a river or lake, seeking exactly the right feather. That's another day free from their bothering you will have, for sure. You can also request them to find and select some of these (not everyday, thus time-consuming to acquire) items as ritual equipment: seven fresh oyster shells, five pieces of rose Quartz, a piece of Amber with a visible insect within, a crescent-moon-shaped mirror, a piece of jewellery featuring a Dove motif, some Celtic knotwork - preferably as a woodcarving....

Add all manner of other stuff to suit your own assessment of the likely ease of finding it locally. Once you have had a break, due to your client being busy acquiring the stuff, devise a ritual to use all of the collected items. That is where the magic will really kick in, as the rite will be unique, and the client will have invested so much of themselves in the ingredients, that it has a massive gnosis turbocharger just waiting to kick in....

Of course devising rites which play on the 28-day menstrual-sexual cycle and the lunar cycle, thus requiring repetition each night for a month will also guarantee to keep your client off the phone to you at a given time each night for 4 weeks, which can be blessed relief sometimes.

There are no specimen rites given here, deliberately, but the above hints will allow you to craft something that does the trick of getting the client off your back, and if in the process they manage to divest themselves of some intense and scary neediness they might even score with a partner.

Take your fee in advance of any result, in any case.

Poppets and Image Magick

Image magick is a very simple and hugely effective way to cast spells. Poppets can be made in the 'traditional' way, from melting wax and then moulding it while it cools, or painted on stone ...as in the image, something we found washed up on a beach in Eastern Spain, debris churned up by a recent storm, from an ancient and now flooded undersea Villa, and which stylised human shape we used for some useful and very potent image magic for a while, until it was 'retired', being worn out after a hectic flurry of spellcasting, and it then became part of a senescent garden rockery.

However in a modern world that is chock-full of proprietary human images, there are many other simple and effective options for the 'base' structure which can then be personalized or linked with your target in whatever way; including:

Making ice, marzipan or pastry poppets using a 'gingerbread man' mould bought from a cookery shop (as in the picture, you can buy the full body shape or just heads).

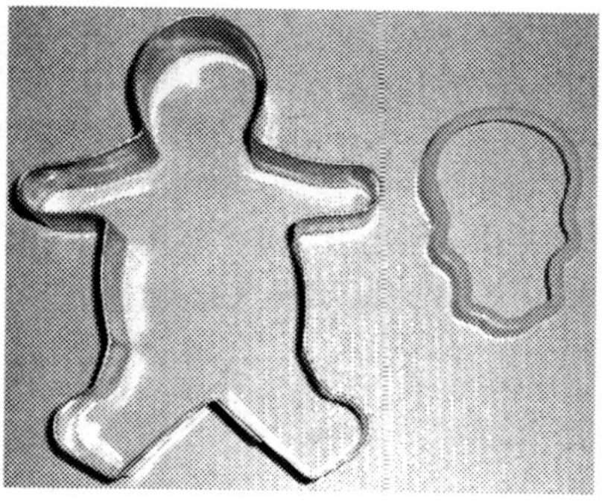

You could also try employing an 'Action Man', 'GI Joe', 'Ken' or 'Barbie' doll (® all trademarks we expect), and do note that the use of power drills or heated nails may be required for facilitating any malefic magickal acts which need anything to be inserted through the hard plastic.

We have seen a Barbie spontaneously 'baptised' with the name of a target and then smashed to pieces with magical intent, using a clawhammer, which act was rather splendidly 'immediate' as magic goes, but it may be that your needs are slightly more refined.

Most dolls of this kind do not have obvious genitalia, by the way (presumably to stop children-at-play asking various questions that may embarrass some adults), so if the spell is in any way related to the sexual organs (be that for healing or harming) you will need to make something to symbolise this - perhaps using child's modeling clay - for which one trademark in the UK is '*Plasticine*'. Uncooked bread dough or flour and water paste will also work for this purpose.

It is also quite simple to carve a poppet from well-cooled lard or butter, identify it with the target, imbue it with an intent, then leave it in the sunshine to melt. Judicious application of a magnifying glass to any part of the anatomy would give extra, focused effect if desired. We have seen a very powerful magnifying glass used on a hot day to quite brutally and rapidly 'laserbeam off' the head of one such poppet, with much 'James-Bond-villain'-esque cackling as a suitably dark and unpleasant accompaniment to the act. Not a healing rite, obviously....

Plastic toy soldiers (and other small toy figures) also make reasonably useful poppets...or for works of destruction, a lead soldier can be linked to the target, named and then placed on a hot charcoal disk (the kind used to burn magical incense powders in many-a-ritual) where it will slowly melt and collapse into an unrecognisable pool of metal. Once cooled the amorphous piece of lead can be ritually cast into running water with a pinch of salt for total banishment, or shot out to sea (or into a deep lake) using a catapult. Note that molten lead fumes are very toxic - so accomplish the melting part of the act outdoors (or with really good ventilation if indoors) or you may induce a death gnosis in yourself. If you survive, some brain damage may result.

Talking of poisons, various plant stems can be woven into images when you make them, be they poisonous plants or healing types, or if creating poppets from lard or butter you can mix in ground-up spices etc to suit your intent - a book of correspondences like Crowley's 777 or a standard Herbal text will be of great use there.

If you need (or just want) a life-size poppet, then inflatable sex dolls or clothes-shop mannequins are the way forward. These can be useful for absent healing, or a major cursing when a very obvious focus is needed, or for group work where a smaller poppet may appear insignificant, and thus detract from the power of the work being done. While gnosis from laughter is a very useful form, it is rather counterproductive to the ritual intent if the laughter is *because* of a very poor piece of image-making.

If the work is severely malefic you can hang the thing up somewhere in a remote (and-or soundproof) place, and loudly beat the crap out of it with a selection of sticks, whips, knives, bats and other weapons; which gives a gnostic effect that stamping on a poppet that may only be six inches long can never have.

Some department stores can be persuaded to part with damaged or 'old-fashioned' mannequins for free if you can present a coherent and believable-enough story to them.... Such as that you are an infant school teacher in a profoundly under-funded state school and you need the mannequin to dress up in a historical costume you have made in your own time to make a tableau in order to teach the lovely little underprivileged kids something worthwhile.

With ingenuity you can imagine the kind of convincing sob-story that might just press the 'generosity-buttons' of a jaded shop manager, provided you insist that a broken mannequin will be perfect. A broken one will cost the shop money to dispose of, so you are actually doing them a favour.

A faked letter from a non-existent school will help smooth the way, so practice your computer graphics skills to make up a convincing letterhead, practice your identity-manipulation skills in order to be convincing, and choose an area that is far enough away from your home area and heavily populated enough to be too much trouble to check out for a list of schools. If you succeed, make sure you use the same letterhead to post a thankyou letter to the shop, which leaves your path open to have another mannequin from them a few years later, as it's possible you'll need another one, one day. Given enough sustained beatings, they do eventually wear out....

You may alternatively make a life-size image by a magical variation of the kind of thing that goes on regularly in public demonstrations. Make an effigy of the target using clothes (preferably including at least something of theirs in the construction, which you may have had opportunity to steal earlier, as in the prevention of pursuit ritual) and if your aim is malefic then hang it by the neck, generally beat it up, and (at somewhere suitable) burn it. If benefic, do whatever soothing and calming stuff seems appropriate to the need - actually feeding the effigy with real and 'healthy' food such as fruit can be surprisingly effective as a healing rite, and in group work taking it in turns to stand in close vigil and doing repetitive cleansing rites over the effigy for an entire 24 hour cycle can be incredibly useful for a protective spell.

The popular perception of image magick is of 'voodoo dolls' used for malign purposes, but in reality image magick is as neutral as any other kind. The image you make is irrelevant compared to the intent, and that can be to heal, harm, or simply hold. The use of poppets for setting up binding spells is sadly often overlooked in magick, and is a very handy technique; for example if you want to get to a particular shop before someone else you know, to get your hands on a copy of a certain rare magick book that has become suddenly available... (sorry, James).

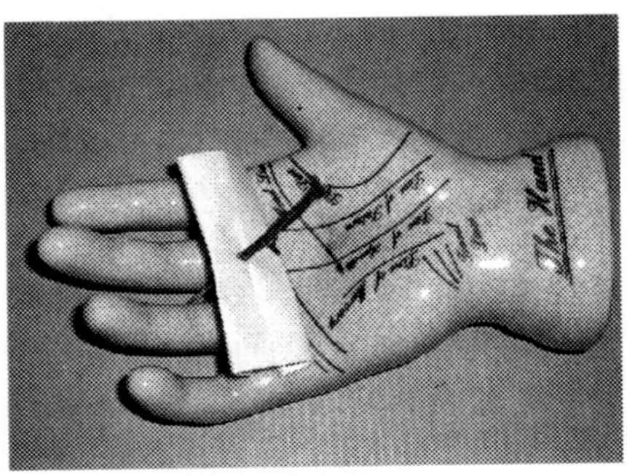

That is an example of some very simple Image Magic as a binding spell - a hand-drawn image of a person is folded, pierced with a thorn that does not actually enter the drawn image, but holds the paper closed, and given to a hand - a cheap china palmistry hand in this case, but a glove stuffed with cotton wool will also be fine, 'to hold' for a time.

Of course if you are remotely able to sew, a 'traditional' poppet made of cloth is great, this one below uses a shop-bought doll face (with additional painting, done under intent) for added effect, and is shown here just prior to being sewn up after a written spell and various linking articles were placed in the neck.

This one was used for a while, and is now in store, still with a crossbow arrow embedded in the thorax, as the work on that one continues.

Ice, Ice Baby

The mention of ice above reminds us of a quickie ritual, which can be done when there is snow or ice around in the outside world.

Since ice melts in a reasonably short time, a sigil constructed of ice or snow (or indeed a poppet in the form of a snowman) can be very effective for a 'timed' piece of work in a desired location, and one that leaves no visible trace once the thaw comes.

In frosty conditions a sigil can also be traced onto a car windscreen or bonnet with your finger[11].

Or if you are defrosting your home freezer you can use the residual ice attached to the inside for the same purpose.

11 American readers take that as 'windshield' and 'hood', respectively.

'It's The Icing on the Cake'

One does not have to be a master chef or even show any great culinary competence in order to make and decorate cakes nowadays. Most large stores will sell fairly foolproof ready-mixed packets, which only need you to add water. Alternatively one can buy instant biscuit-cookie mix, and shaped dough cutters, so the ingenuity required is only extended as far as being able to turn on an oven and read a clock.

If any level of cookery is beyond you, plenty of shops will sell you a plain iced cake.

Regardless of whether you cooked it yourself for not, take your cake or biscuits and start designing. Many sigils and magickal designs can be drawn, using pre-prepared icing in tubes (which comes in all manner of colours), which look a little like toothpaste tubes. Experiment as ye will, and use the cakes to eat, taking the intent of an appropriate sigil into your own body, and nourishing both your flesh and self. As a consequence of biology it is then excreted a while later, so a sigil for cleansing or purging of something you no longer wish to be part of you would be a particularly appropriate method here.

If the work is of a nature where the 'purged thing' needs to be returned to the cause, for example an ex-lover who is causing you grief, then don't use the flush handle of your toilet. Make the cake, eat it, wait around 24 hours and crap into a plastic bag; the contents of which can be surreptitiously dumped under cover of night in a quiet and secluded corner of the target's garden, minus the plastic bag. As always, do this with magickal intent, and be aware that human shit can be DNA-typed if it is found and the recipients are annoyed enough (or important enough) to be able to get the cops involved, so reserve this method only for spells that you absolutely must do, not those you think it would merely be nice, or amusing, to do.

Or, for more bleak purposes, place the entire sigilised cake, uneaten, in a wild place to rot away, thus taking the intent of the sigil into the realm of decay and dissolution as the cake is destroyed and consumed by one or more of the ground, weather conditions, bacteria and any local wildlife.

If the cake is to be eaten, and you have the requisite culinary skills, then a little special herb in the cake mix can aid the meditative gnosis immensely, as can a drop of your own blood, or sexual fluids, added to the mixing bowl. For those entertaining and adventurous psychonauts with any fungal expertise and a suitable location in which to eat the cake and the time to appreciate the effects, the addition of a considered and calculated dose of miscellaneous psilocybes to the cake mixture, and taking care not to cook at too hot a temperature (which inactivates the effect, or so we hear) can also be of great magickal use for attaining a Gnostic and focused state.

Once the cake has been portioned out to those present, ensure you have some *other* items of food around in case there is an attack of 'the munchies'... or you may lose a few days to a whirl of creative chaos. Which can be fun, but slightly less so if entirely unplanned.

Obviously, if any of the above suggestions regarding cake ingredients are illegal acts in your location then you simply must not do them.

Obviously.

As a variation of the use of wildlife to spread a spell; using 'bird seed' such as is sold to feed caged pet birds to make a sigil on the ground can be very effective, as wild birds will fly down, eat their fill and fly away, latterly to shit the remnants of the seed over a very wide area of surrounding country, so as usual, choose the intent wisely, as it will be activated over miles, by a very large battalion, supplied free of charge by nature.

If you have a target whose home you cannot get into to secrete anything magickal, a sigil carved on a piece of cheese or a sausage, and thrown to a domestic dog or cat in your target's garden is also a way to ensure that your intent is taken into their premises, and probably defecated out of the animal in the same location. If you are really lucky the pet will actually vomit the mess up inside the house.

While we are eating, it is also quite fun to do some standard 'knot magic' using edible liquorice-style string. Knot magic traditionally uses three knots, which involve increasing amounts of magical force. For example the intent might be to recover stolen property, so knot one might be tied with the intent that the police catch the thief and your property is returned. Knot two might be tied with the intent that the thief meets with some nasty accident and is moved to return your property out of some guilt-fear association with the accident. Knot three might be tied with the intent that the thief dies a horrible death and whoever goes through their stuff realises that some of it is yours and returns it. A dramatic example, but it gives a good picture of the kind of progression involved. Using standard rope the spells are set-off working by untying the knots at intervals, and waiting for the effect. Using edible string, one can eat the knot and give it a good chewing to set it working. The edible string version allows one to actually take-in the intent as a sacrament, too, so the knot magic method can be used for three-stage works of strengthening and self-healing in that way.

Invisibility One-Oh-One (Smoke and Mirrors)

As a Chaos Cunner you might sometimes wish to be rather public for paying clients, however you may also need to be 'invisible' to selected persons, as useful camouflage for the real high weirdnesses that your personal magick is producing in the world, so it is sometimes necessary to employ some misdirection.

This can vary. Examples would include an absolute and categorical denial that the strange happenings are anything to do with you, which might not be believed, especially if you have had a few very public successes, or some very pleased clients who are telling all their friends about your incredible abilities to tamper with the fabric of consensus reality.

You can thus take the precaution of making even weirder things happen locally, so that the real magick goes unnoticed below the info-smokescreen of weirdnesses.

Try things like:

Regularly leave an interesting book in a telephone box and put a small pile of loose change on the top of a wall in a public place at pedestrian eye-height, along with a single, wrapped chocolate. This will cause strange local gossip with a matter of only a few repetitions.

Periodically leave a geometric arrangement of squashed ping-pong balls on a park bench, with a half-used jar of mustard, a small denomination coin and a drinking straw.

Leave a floppy disk containing a link to your favourite bizarre website in a taxi, train or on a bus, held in the hand of a small child's doll, that is blindfolded. Or gagged.

Wearing gloves to avoid transferring your fingerprints, buy a newspaper and cut all the capital letters from the front page. Leave the cut-up newspaper, rolled up, wrapped with gift paper, and tied with red ribbon, on a bus or train. Print out an address label and use it to mail all the capitals back to the newspaper offices, using an anonymous posting box in a busy street, with an anonymous typed note saying **"I am returning these in case you run out, you seem to use a lot of them each day"**.

Repeat this weekly, it will seriously mess with people's heads.

Type out some short and varied suicide notes and carry them with you. When you see roadkill animals, leave one note with each, perhaps clasped plaintively in a claw or paw....

Wear a wristwatch on each arm, set to different (and both wildly incorrect) times. When someone asks you for the time, hold out both arms, look at them both, show them to the querent, frown, and say **"I'm really sorry, I simply don't know"**. Walk away, shaking your head and muttering incoherently. If you are agile enough, you could add a third watch (also inaccurate) to one ankle, so you could look at that too, to check the other watches.

Once you have done this a few times, a few people will probably start copying your actions, thinking you are some kind of street performer, and-or in the hope that they might be on camera (Gods bless 'Reality TV' shows for making everyone be prepared to do anything to get their 15 minutes of fame), especially if they are students, to whom 'wacky' things are most appealing.

Be very obvious about wearing a 'hands free' earpiece and microphone for your mobile (cell) phone. This gives you license to walk around in public having conversations with yourself about anything, or giving a not entirely correct commentary on your surroundings, out loud. Make up some items that are not there, or some things that are simply not happening, to tell your imaginary phone caller about. This will make people in the same street think their own perceptions of the environment are wrong, and make them confused. Leave the cellphone switched off during all of this, of course.

Write letters to your local press remarking on local strange events, that simply did not actually happen - a magazine such as *Fortean Times* (or similar 'bizarre happenings' websites) will be a most useful source material for such odd things that have happened elsewhere - simply take an example of one of their news reports, alter some peripheral details, embellish it with a nearby location and send the story in to your local press, to the 'Readers Letters' page.

Do this often enough, and invariably, other correspondents will write in, trying to outdo your tales with those of their own, making the 'average reader' shake their head in disbelief. You could also write in mentioning the strange things that have been occurring lately, involving finding ping-pong balls and mustard etc, as mentioned above; providing that nobody else has already done so. Above all, be creative, and lie your damn head off... that dog you nearly ran over last week was huge, with red eyes, someone had dyed most of it green, and it looked like it had a goddamn baby kangaroo in its mouth....

A 21st century Witch Bottle

Witch bottles have been used for centuries for the magickal protection of property and locations. Traditionally they contained all manner of pins, nails, urine, organic materials, animal bones etc. To make your own, take a piss into a bottle, mix a few drops of milk, some of your hair, your nail clippings, your IP address written on paper[12] (if you wish to protect your 'on-line' location as well), and microwave it for 10 seconds... while it is still hot, add a pinch of dressmaking pins, push in a cork stopper, seal the stopper in with molten wax and ritually bury the bottle in your garden, with intent.

You could perhaps use the same hole in the ground to plant some useful medicinal, culinary or entheogenic shrub, which by your later physical ingestion of the produce makes a magical link that reinforces the protective effects of the witch bottle. Do not disturb the bottle again. Renew this procedure every few years with a new bottle and a new plant, or whenever you move house.

The same basic idea can also be employed for offensive magick.

Having first made your own protection bottle, try this addition for stubborn or noxious problems with others. Take another empty bottle, preferably of a drink that was in some way substandard or inferior, such as very cheap bitter 'plonk' wine, or a wine that had 'corked' or otherwise gone bad in some form. Add to it a selection of bent pins and needles.

Add a 'magickal link', such as the handwriting of the target (or the butt of a cigarette which they have smoked, or some of their hair covertly taken from a pillow or hairbrush, if you have had email from them then take *their* IP address and write it down... you get the idea), and speak your intent out loud. A very useful link can be made if you know your target's physical address, use the internet to procure a map of their street (for example multimap.com)

12 How to find your IP address and what it is – the IP is a set of numbers that whoever provides your internet service will automatically assign to your computer. It is a little like a very specific Postal or ZIP Code. To find out yours, simply write an email and send it to yourself. Then open the email, and depending on what email programme you use, look at the Properties or Header section of the menu, and you should be given a number of the form 214.46.20.176 (which is a fabricated one by the way). Use that number as an online identifier for the protective bottle.

and add a printout of that to the bottle.

Add a selection of small quantities of various noxious fluids that can be readily found in the average household: such as vinegar, bleach, detergent, scouring cream, very hot curry sauce etc.

Unpleasant 'found items' such as dogshit, dead slugs or small pieces of roadkill animals add a certain Lovecraftian slimy ambience to the mix, too.

Optional items might include fish-hooks, 'foreign' coins (being 'useless' in your country the uselessness will be transmitted to the target as a feeling of futility or similar), peppercorns, any food that has 'gone off' (especially rotting fish) and which cannot be eaten, used and thus 'dead' matches, small pieces of broken glass etc.

Do this while giving a spoken 'running commentary' about how the symbolism of each ingredient will adversely affect the target, for example while adding vinegar "may their piss be like vinegar from henceforth", for scouring powder "may their skin be forever rough", for fishing hooks "may the barbs of fate tear their flesh" etc.... Mix well...watching out not to splash *yourself with the foul brew, and* **avoid breathing in the miasma emanating from the bottle.**

Firmly insert a cork and take the item outside to somewhere safe... despite the small quantities of each chemical in use the mix of bleach and suchlike may cause production of gas, so a strip or two of strong 'Gaffer' tape (aka Duct tape) firmly bound over the cork (or some wire twisted up around the stopper, like on the top of a champagne bottle) may be sensible in order to keep it in the bottle. In any case place the bottle in a closed dustbin or similar with a brick on the lid to hold it in, so that if it does actually explode then the flying glass doesn't hurt anyone that you care about, or leave any mess. Laugh out loud.

Allow the bottle to brew for a while, preferably overnight, then carefully wrap it in a few layers of cardboard and take the thing away somewhere safe (a quarry, a waste tip, a builders' skip or dumpster, a bottle recycling bank, a disused well or mine-shaft, an abandoned building) where it can be safely thrown and smashed, again, with a magickal intent. Exit from the scene, laughing.

If your local architecture allows, ritually embed a brand new and very sharp knife just below the surface of some new concrete outside your front door, point outwards, to repel unwanted influences. Similarly, you can bury all kinds of magickal stuff; spells that you wish to 'fix' in a location for whatever purpose, in major construction sites by the simple matter of throwing it over the fence in early evening after the workmen have gone, but while the concrete foundations you are aiming the item for are still wet, so the item sinks into it before it has time to set. Best items are sigils inscribed on fairly heavy stones of less than 3 inches diameter, which sink well if you time the throw right with when the concrete was poured, usually with a satisfying 'plop'.

Horse skulls were often buried or secreted in buildings as a protective, fetishistic charm in Britain. To save the trouble and extreme mess of taking a real horse's head off, use a *My Little Pony*™ head for the same thing in yours - anoint it with perfumed oils, bless it, have a short 'whinnying and snorting conversation' with it to tell it what you want it to achieve, have an exhausting pretend gallop around your house with it to charge it with protective force and a bit of gnosis, then secrete it under floorboards or bury it under something at the threshold of your door.

What about paying customers?

Cunning folk were, it seems, often gifted storytellers, so the modern jobbing chaos cunner needs to at least know some good dirty jokes and witty anecdotes as a diversion for the client before the required and requested magick is performed. It then makes a ritually-useful contrast to become deadly serious, poker-faced and unblinking both during the rite *and* when any bill for the work done is later presented to them....

Make up a receipt and business card design using a nice piece of Goetic-looking or just plain Goat-looking, sorcerous imagery - tradition sells, especially on receipts or business cards.

It is vital that you steadfastly refuse to take on the vast majority of the magickal work people want you to do; since nothing succeeds like appearing to be exclusive - if you will obviously whore your talents out to anyone at a moment's notice then you seem as nothing.

When you do actually deign to accept work to do from someone, only slightly subtly make it clear that you are doing them a really huge favour to fit their minor needs into your hectic schedule and that you have a lifestyle that they simply could not conceive of (without giving any details - an air of mystery sells too). Do not be available for them on the first date or time that they suggest for a meeting to discuss their needs.

You must not appear to be in any way an employee; you are a 'consultant' and they are incredibly lucky and privileged to be spared any of your immensely valuable time from your schedule.

Oh yeah!

To confuse, or remove someone's insight

The need to metaphorically 'blind' an opponent or adversary is often something that will arise. While they cannot 'see', you are at liberty to act in whatever way is required, unobserved. To achieve this, take a small mirror (decorative mirror tiles from a hardware shop are good for this, and cheap - if you find them on a 'sale' or 'offer' price, buy a load....) draw a designed sigil on it with black (or dark-coloured) nail varnish or paint, preferably involving a sigil or glyph for the target's name, within an eye symbol that is crossed through. Allow this to dry overnight.

Take the mirror to somewhere high that is above very hard ground, or 'concreted' such as a high-rise car park, a bridge or climb a tall tree. Achieve gnosis by whichever way suits the intent, and then activate the sigil by dropping the mirror off the side, while rapidly repeating the target's name and focusing your intent upon them until the mirror hits the ground, at which point laugh loudly and with feeling. Leave the area immediately, choosing your exit route from having paid attention beforehand to where any security cameras are located if you use an urban setting, as the smashing noise may draw attention to 'something untoward going on'.

Again, use a bit of common sense - do this early morning or late at night, and in such a way that you do not drop the mirror on anyone and kill them.

In case you are caught on security camera, mask your actions by appearing to be having a cigarette break or making a cell-phone call while actually leaning against the parapet wall and activating the mirror sigil. Dress anonymously, in the common garb of the area so that any blurry security camera image could be mistaken for anyone else. Keep your cellphone actually turned off during all of this as the authorities can track phones to within a few hundred metres in space and a matter of seconds in time if they know the phone number and have the will to start checking call records.

The thief of Dr John Dee's magickal crystal from a London museum in 2004 was caught on surveillance camera, but he or she was indistinguishable in many ways apart from a long black leather coat; which shows a superb understanding of this method of blending into the scenery.... Since the film *The Matrix* was first released the preponderance of long leather coats in society has increased drastically, which makes them wonderful camouflage, as they have become almost a uniform for people of a certain age (and us older ones who still wear them from a previous time when they were fashionable, if not the time before, these things tending to run in cycles)[13]. If you wish to be invisible, be unremarkable in appearance first; it is a damn good start....

Handy Hint:

There are many types of behaviour of an 'everyday' nature that can be used to mask magickal acts.

The include things like ...looking through binoculars at a distant landscape while actually meditating with closed eyes or formulating a visualised sigil in your head ... lighting a cigarette as a mask for a 'coughing' or spitting spell, when you have sigilised a desire into something that can be turned into a guttural noise, which is quickly 'spat out' as a noise, disguised as mundane coughing ....

13 No, we don't know who stole the Dee crystal.

The Sex-S & M Gnosis

You thought this was a new thing? Read this, in a symbolic frame of mind:

From Ben Jonson's *The Masque of Queens*, date: 'olden times'

The Spindle is now a-turning; The Moone it is red, and the starres are fled, But all the sky is a burning: The Ditch is made, and or nayles the spade, With pictures full, of waxe, and of wooll: Theyr livers WE stick, with needles quick There lacks but the blood, to make vp the flood. Quickly Dame then, bring yor part in, Spur, spur, upon little Martin, Merely, merely, make him sayle, A worme in his mouth and a thorne in's tayle, Fire above, and fire below, With a Whip i' your hand, to make him goe, O, now, shee's come! Let all be dumbe.

The words *may* be interpreted as being Spindle (wooden dildo, or just a cock), Red moon (menstrual magick), Stars fled (darkness - perhaps as a code for anal sex), Burning sky (the 'flashing' coloured astral visions experienced during full-on sexual magick), Ditch made (vagina open), Nail (slang for penis), Spade (alludes to burial, in 'the ditch-vagina'); this rite can be used to charge a poppet (a figure of wax, wearing woollen clothes) which can then be used for malefic magic, and it works better when it is then charged by 'woman on top' sex (riding, and the spurring on imagery) followed by anal and oral sex (worm in mouth, thorn in tail), which produces sexual-magickal kundalini fire from top to bottom. The rite ends with some good old whipping gnosis until a final orgasm, which simply silences everyone present with its intensity.

There are probably any number of alternative and more literary readings of the piece, this is just a thought... there are no 'right answers', but do remember that 'good and dirty' sex is simply awesome for the purposes of reaching gnosis, since it challenges taboos and has a mighty effect on the consciousness.

Handy Hint:

Clothes do NOT maketh the man (or woman) but society does react in different ways to how we are dressed. Taking a small sum of money, investigate your local charity and thrift shops, and devise yourself an entirely new image, for not very much money. Experiment with how the world perceives you while you are outside in your new outfit, and observe reactions of various people.

From various experiments and repetitions of this exercise you can gradually devise a magick-themed wardrobe, dressing according to how you wish the world to behave towards you. It also gets one away from the stereotypical image of chaos magicians always just wearing black.... Yeah, it's a slimming colour, but it can be very dull too.

Be fabulous while you are doing it all, in any case.

Be sure to accessorise!

Beltane, Sex and Gnosis

Many neo pagans seem to become more public and noticeable around the end of April (in the northern hemisphere, anyhow), the 'traditional' festival of Beltane. When attending group rituals one often finds many more people present at this one than any other, perhaps because of the element of fertility and fecundity implicit in both the wider world and echoed in neo pagan ritual at this time of year - it may be that many a solitary pagan feels that this might be the time to meet a prospective sexual partner after a long winter of frantic masturbation, or perhaps not.

In any case, the sexual longing implicit in the aethyrs surrounding such a gathering can be most useful magical food for a good chaos cunner, and it can also be a time to give a most commendable public display in ritual. Even averagely-done magick is pretty close to the buzz from really good sex in any case, and the 'current' of the symbolic deity-form at this time of year, whether you call it Pan, Herne or something else, can be most invigorating, and enlightening. A week or so before Beltane (usually this is May 1st , but local customs vary) sit down quietly and attempt to 'tune in' to the approaching current, using whatever meditational aids or substances you see fit to use, and record what happens.

The results of one such experiment follow: with only slight tweaking of the original channelled version, and it proved to be of immense power when recited during a large group rite, after which, had we been of a mind to indulge[14], several pretty likely (and in one case, positively *dripping*) new sexual partners approached us over the course of the next hour or so. They were hugely impressed by the immense magickal 'charge' which our participation and these words gave to the ritual, and they were all most certainly 'moist with anticipation':

My names are many: Herne, Cernunnos and others
My name is not important, I am merely a messenger
The message is Awake! Awake! AWAKE!
Return to full life within this mortal world!
Feel the earth awaken, breathe the soft air

14 At the time, we were not; nothing personal to those making themselves available, one of whom was particularly hot.

Arise! Arise! ARISE! You children of creation
For now your land is alive again
The stars have turned full circle, the wheel is bringing you to spring-time once more

You are renewed with the earth, you are open to healing and regeneration, with every opportunity of life before you
The opportunity to do what thou wilt, and to BE what thou wilt

I carried the ashes from summer's burning, through autumn and through winter's cold
Those ashes are now the soil to nourish your hopes through spring

To bring you back to the summer magic, and wonders to behold
Awake and arise, AWAKE AND ARISE with health love and happiness, from the spirit of the Greenwood

So mote it be!

Sympathetic Magick

The doctrine of signatures was much-used in the herbalism and medical practices of yore[15]; for example the plant called Lungwort was believed to be useful as a curative aid for respiratory ailments, it looked a bit like a cross-section of a lung, and so it was named as such[16].

Gathering herbs for various purposes, culinary or sorcerous can be a very magickal act anyhow, and if possible use a one-handed pair of 'sheep shears' for the purpose, not just because it looks sinister to the client (see image below). For some reason these things tend to inspire dread in folk. If we didn't loathe Freudianism so much we would suggest it was perhaps due to some kind of castration anxiety, but we find that many women go weak at the knees when they see this piece of equipment in action too, so it can't all be due to cutting-off of stuff fears.

Use of this piece of equipment actually makes life easy as there is a free hand to gather the herbs, and the repetitive metallic swish-swish noise of the blades can be used for encouraging gnosis.

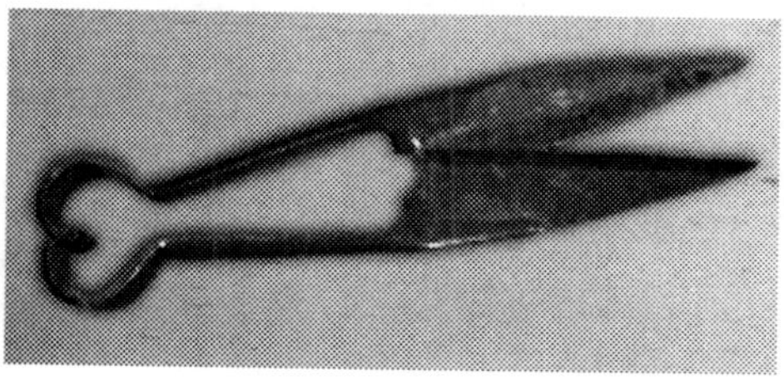

The same doctrine of signatures can hold true in other cases, provided one wishes to make such a magical link - for example, have you noticed how some people are intimately involved with wearing certain designer labels....

15 For those needing a date, 'the first day of Yore' comes at the exact halfway point between "distant past" and "long, long ago".

16 Refer to any old-provenanced Herbal, such as Culpepper's, which has been around since the 1600s, and is still in print.

Handy Hint:

Combine magical weapons in unusual permutations wherever possible.

For example, a walking stick that is ritually consecrated as a wand, or a credit card consecrated as a knife can be very useful, but there are many more examples.

A female chaos mage of our acquaintance puts a ritually-charged powder compact mirror and a consecrated lipstick to quite terrifying magical uses, and it always looks like all she is doing it touching up her lip colour....

Lateral thinking is a vital tool for the modern sorcerer, and having a tool that looks like one thing but that does the job of something else as well means you have less stuff to carry around, and you are carrying things that are far less conspicuous than ritual swords and elaborate robes, if you need to be un-noticed...

Shot through the heart…

A traditional protective charm is made from the heart of an animal stuck through with pins, so either buy one from a butcher or make a symbol of one. If you go for the real meat article, tell the butcher it's **"for my dog"** and have a name, gender, age, breed and some simple 'amusing puppy behaviour' anecdotes like shoe-chewing and floor-shitting behaviour for the animal fabricated beforehand, in case anyone in the shop asks.

Or, to make a symbolic form, use a large piece of that stiff plastic foam[17] which can be acquired from a florists' supply or handicrafts shop. Cut it into the rough shape of a heart, soak it in animal blood taken from some very raw meat and ritually thrust hatpins, nails, skewers or kitchen knives into it to your heart's content, (pun certainly intended) visualising your intent most strongly as the blood runs down the implement onto your arms.

It really doesn't matter if the foam material is not cut to what you consider to be a geometrically correct heart shape as physiologically, hearts are simply not 'heart-shaped', as you will see if you buy an animal's one from the butcher. It is the intent with which you do the carving and stabbing that counts.

17 Sometimes called 'oasis', probably a trademark.

Get it taped: practical magic using technology

This method is a verbal, sonic way to produce a sigil, and to set it to work. There have already been some inspiring pieces of writing by others about the use of sound in magic, Jan Fries springs to mind, while Dave Lee and Phil Hine in particular have done some great and inspiring work with recording speech and noise on tape and then playing with that product, using 'cut-up' techniques. Since we cannot suggest any improvement on their rather super specific methods, this piece takes the use of taped sound off into another area of practical work entirely.

Define your desire, in as few words as possible, and without using equivocal phrases. This alone is an act of magic - by defining, and then refining your desire you are setting your deep mind at work on the matter, so subconscious but powerful wheels are already in motion in creating the necessary effect or outcome.

Once you have your succinct desire ready to verbalise, (which will not sound like English, note, due to the abbreviated nature of removing the duplicated letters - as explained in the sigilising instructions given earlier) pick a new, blank audiotape (which has been bought without haggling, as the old magic books would say), unwrap it, put it in a recorder and tape-record yourself speaking the succinct desire aloud. And MEANING it. Repeat the desire as many times as you see fit, which may be any number, including just once, and then stop the tape - do NOT rewind. Remove the tape from the machine, and take the cassette apart - some cassettes are held together with very small screws; others are simply glued, but in either case break the cassette open, like an egg (a hint for symbolism).

The amount of tape which has been used will be much the smaller of the two little reels that you have in your hands (unless you turned your desire into a really very long mantra indeed), so it should be obvious which of the reels will only contain silence. Or the absence of sound, if you want to be really picky. Cut the tape, and discard the silent reel.

The reel containing your expressed desire is now the object of a ritual. Harking back to the blow job-wind method (above), the natural 'magical' elements are perfect for empowering the spell. Depending on your particular desire, choose the most pertinent element to suit the outcome, and work with the tape as suits:

For Earth - wind the tape solemnly around a very large rock - a rock with the authority and power of earth, and intimating the immensity and potentiality of geological periods of time - this would suit a long, progressive desire, and so should remain wrapped around the stone for at least an hour, allowing the magnetic fields of the rock and the tape to merge, while you meditate upon the desire and achieve gnosis, before removing the tape from the stone and disposing of it responsibly. It would be nice to say "wrap the tape around a standing stone or stone in a henge" and leave it there for good - but the very act of leaving it there might easily cause damage to the stone (and the often centuries-old lichens growing on it), cause trouble for subsequent magicky visitors to the site and as such is not worth it, for any desire[18]. You could also wrap the tape around the roots of a shrub or tree which you are about to plant, and bury it if the sigilised desire is of a nurturing or 'growth' nature.

For Fire - this would suit a banishing, or particularly energetic desire - drape the loops of tape over either a metal trident, such as a mediaeval demonologist would have... or, in the absence of that, a garden fork or one of those long-handled doodads that come in tool-sets for barbecues. Light a small fire. Outdoors! When the fire is burning well, hang the tape over it - as high as you can safely reach, and slowly bring it down into the flames.

As the tape changes state, so is the desire released to find fruition. As the tape burns it will become molten, and that molten plastic can cause nasty burns, so unless you wish to (perhaps permanently) sigilise your skin too, keep clear of the dripping molten material, the smoke from which may well be toxic if inhaled, too. These 2 possible dangers could be incorporated into any desire with which you use this method, of course. You could also use the dripping molten material to anoint a visual sigilised version of

18 For some useful hints on how to magickally work sympathetically, and without damage, in ancient monuments see the ASLAN charter online (the site has moved home a few times, so search on Google™ for the latest location).

the very same desire you have just made in tape, with that visual sigil being inscribed on wood, stone or metal. Allow the dripping molten material to obscure the visual sigil, and you have a beautifully locked-'paired' sigil there....

For Water - find a flowing, preferably FAST-flowing piece of water, and a place where you can reach out into the current, such as a footbridge, bend in the river or stream, or from a jetty or a boat. Tie a cork or small piece of wood on one end of the tape, and throw that out into the current - and unreel the tape as the wood/cork is carried swiftly downstream.... At the second at which the full extent of the tape is (literally) 'played out' into the water, the spell is cast.

Don't leave the tape in the water as it's the kind of litter that can really do damage to wildlife, especially water birds such as swans and ducks. And doing that may make your love-spell client's job (see above) in finding a Swan feather much easier, they will just have to follow the smell of dead creature. Roll it up and dispose of it elsewhere safely - once the sigil is sent out the tape is merely mundane rubbish in any case, and need not be retained. This method can be tailored for particular spells if you are able to work it upstream of the 'target', be that a person, an institution, a location.

If it has a target at all... it could be used on yourself where a particular desire is put into a stream or river which runs into the reservoir that ultimately feeds the domestic water supply to your town, and thus your own home, so it will act to charge up all of your baths, cups of tea etc for the future....

One slight problem with this method in recent years is that since the 'war on terror' started we gather that reservoirs are under considerably more security cover than they used to be, in case some mythical baddie is moved to throw in a bucket of nerve poisons. However 'more patrolled than they used to be' comes from a starting point of virtually zero, in our experience, so it should not be hard to perform this rite unmolested in a suitable place somewhere further upstream.

On a more immediate level, and for direct personal effect it could also be used directly under the taps as you are running a bath, or hung under a shower head.

For Air - choose a high spot on a windy day, make a small kite - just a diamond of light cardboard is enough, and 'fly' the kite. As with the water working, when the full length of the recorded tape is unreeled by the elements, the spell is cast. Again, dispose of the tape afterwards sensibly.

As will have occurred to some, video tapes, although a little wider and heavier (and thus harder to fly with) can be used for many of the same purposes, and this medium is particularly useful for banishment and holding spells when the subject of the spell is captured (again, a literal word) on the video. With the right technology and a little bit of editing, a suitable visual spell could be placed around them on the tape that is used. This method would be of especially use if you wished to work any magic on someone who had made a television appearance, for those who wish to dabble in political or celebrity magicks, for example, or to work a spell against anyone who might have been recorded on home videotape. The recent cheapening of digital cameras with a short video capability is also a boon to this kind of working, as the result can be simply edited using cheap or free-for-download software, and the results burned onto compact disc, which are then used in a similar manner to the tape.

We are not *Illuminates of Thanateros* members[19] but one of their conventions that we especially like is to classify their published (and internally-circulated) workings as either tested or untested. Most of the above is conceptual, and thus, in IOT terms, "untested". However the works that have been done practically have been most effective, from which the rest has been extrapolated - and so we offer this as a potential working method to those with the Will to experiment.

Since a version of this article first appeared online a correspondent, who I shall call here *GD*, kindly writes to us about "an adaptation that occurred to me. Namely tying the tape fragment to the front mesh of the large fan in my living room in the manner of a prayer flag and pointing it towards an open window. The sound this makes varies for each tape obviously,

19 Never having both had the time and been in one place long enough to undergo the 6-month Neophyte period. One day, maybe...

and I 'listen' to the tape as I meditate in the breeze", which is a superb additional idea, and we thank them for sharing a lovely piece of creative chaos.

The alert reader will have realised that there are some similar possibilities of use for this method onto recordable compact discs as well, with the added effect that CDs are highly reflective, so they could be used as a magic mirror to 'flash' the sun into an indoor location, perhaps the building where the target lives, using the sunlight to carry the spell from the CD. Being so thin the CD could also be slipped into tiny cracks around the threshold of a target's house, under paving stones in the target's garden path, under roof tiles if their roof can easily be reached, for example if they live in a bungalow or some olde worlde style house with low eaves.

The CDs burn very *well*, too:

Divination

As promised above, here are some more divinatory methods. An old method of divination, once common across northern Europe, uses shears, a horticultural sieve and some animal bones, which are cast, a little like *I Ching* sticks. Quite how to do this work seems to vary with each account we read, so we believe there is no right way, and in true Chaos Cunner style we can only suggest that you acquire the material equipment, or some equivalent shaped items (perhaps large scissors, a bowl and pencils of various sizes and colours) and play with the method, to see what works for you.

You could perhaps use the shapes formed by the fallen bones or pencils as visual prompts for the divination, or subdivide the four parts of the sieve marked out by the blades and handles as having particular meanings for particular questions. It is up to you!

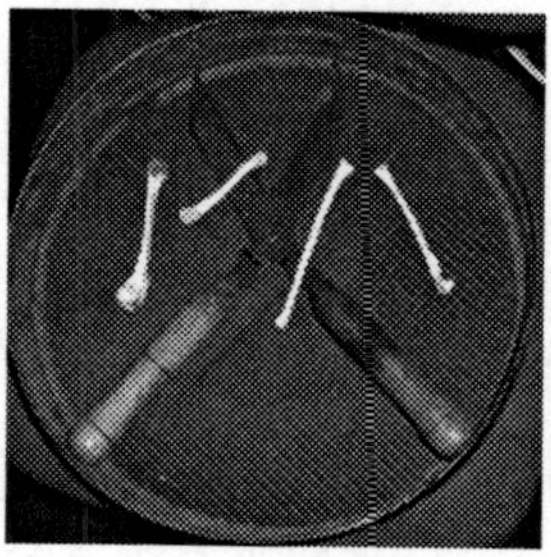

The exact equipment as in the photograph might seem hard or impractical to acquire, however we should remark how damn impressive it can be in the 21st century to produce arcane gardening tools and a bag-ful of bones in front of your client, to show what an old-school sorcerer you really are....

There are many other ways to divine of course, limited only by your ability to invent them:

Scrying into Black Vodka is pretty impressive. One can either use the manufactured Black Vodka, or the slightly cheaper clear stuff with a few drops of black food colouring added. Having a few drops of the colouring already secreted in the bottom of the glass before you pour can also be used for a slight 'wow' effect, as you pour a clear liquid into a seemingly empty glass in sight of the client, and it immediately turns black, to which YOU do not react at all, such sinister transubstantiations being a daily event to you, and thus unremarkable. A carnival trick for sure, but a lot of good magic can be initial trickery to 'prime' the client for 'magickal' things to happen, so it's very useful on that level.

Under very low ambient light and in silence, scry into a shot-glass full of the stuff for as long as seems necessary (you will know when - gnosis will arrive) and then drink down the glass in one go, with intent, before gasping out your message from the liminal world to the client in a suitably dramatic fashion.

An alternative scrying fluid is a drop of oil on water, and use oil that has just been on skin - for example a drop of 'baby oil', the skin-conditioning stuff used by many mothers, taken from an infant if trying to diagnose an illness in them when they are still too young to speak, or a drop of massage oil from an adult who may have an injury that needs some magical input. With this technique the lighting needs to be very low, and set peripherally, in order to pick up the colours produced by oil-on-water.

The internet can be used for randomised divination - look on this as a form of automatic writing using the net. With a word-processor document opened on your computer; close your eyes and type something - anything... it doesn't matter what, just allow your mind to go blank. Do this for a while, until you lose track of what you are typing - even the best touch typist will eventually not be sure that they are producing with this, with their eyes shut.

Repeat this a few times, maybe three times, for three minutes each time, and each time select all the text and delete it without trying to read it. That is your banishing ritual, to empty yourself of your own gibberish. Now the fourth time... close your eyes and wait... then start typing. When it feels right, stop typing and read your words. If they are indeed words at all. Somewhere in your text will be something recognisable as English, probably separated by some complete nonsense. Take the pieces of legible text out and use a search engine like *Google*™, and see what the first 'hit' is for each chunk of words - especially the first *image* hit. This method can be incredibly interesting, and often accurate as a means to find out things that you often cannot even frame a standard divination question for.

Handy Hint:

Eggs from birds can also be used for various magical purposes, such as 'blowing' the egg, painting a face of the target on the blown shell, and using it for whatever purpose of image magic you wish.

Alternatively, do not blow the egg, paint on the face and then find a suitable location in which to ritually smash the egg; with intent. The egg being symbolic of beginnings, this kind of work would be perfect for 'murdering someone's ambitions or dreams'.

"It's all in the EGG !" Practical Kaos Divination

There seems to be considerable ingenuity in the choice of divinatory tools among chaos magicians: using detuned TV sets instead of crystal balls, rapid channel hopping to create a 'cut-up' phrase, scrying in a pool of black vodka (as described above), bibliomancy using any kind of website, trash fiction book or a telephone directory. At some literary altitude above 'trash' we can heartily recommend the works of Clive Barker, whose superb use of imagery and metaphor make his books excellent material for divination.

This would seem to have been much the case with the original cunners, if you couldn't find a 'traditional' black cockerel to kill and read the entrails of, then you made do with something else.... And smartish. It's the results that matter, not the means, and if it was the case that you couldn't do your magic for want of a particular specific piece of kit or ingredient then you'd often not be paid, and go hungry as a result.

We would like to add this method to the growing list of tools for divination. For many generations some indigenous folk-magicians in many countries have been divining by examining the inside of hen's eggs, the amorphous shape of yolk and suchlike providing some subconscious clue on which to base a reading for the client (or ones' self).

A less messy, more fun and chocolate-based version uses 'Kinder Eggs' instead of those laid by a bird. Available from many confectioners, details of the egg themselves can be found here: www.kinder-surprise-eggs.com

For those not familiar with them, the eggs are a foil-wrapped chocolate shell around an opaque plastic canister, which contains an unknown object, one of over 100 kinds of plaything or small game, which requires some element of self-construction.

The chocolate is both dark and milk, emphasising the black-white, yin-yang dichotomy present in all divinatory questions.

A while back, before attending some large group rituals we had taken to buying a large number of these eggs, chosen randomly from the shop shelves, and then once the night's ritual work was done, presenting each participant with a choice of any one of the eggs, after they had formulated a question for the egg to help them answer (thus a doubly-randomised choice, for any statistics buffs reading this).

The chocolate coating provides a pseudo-endorphin rush to the brain and body while the participant opens the canister inside and hopefully finds some meaning in the self-assembly child's toy found within, as well as important distraction and 'earthing' from the night's ritual work.

Results so far have been very interesting indeed, with perhaps the most blatant and amusingly direct answer for one participant being that they found a kit to build a toy crocodile within their chosen egg, and they were thus made fully aware that they had been profoundly snappy to people for the previous few days. Other, deeper and more personal meanings have been found by various participants.

The advantages of this technique over more 'traditional' bird's egg-based methods are that participants get to eat chocolate rather than randomly and messily spreading raw egg yolk and bits of sharp shell all over your temple, the chocolate eggs keep longer than fresh eggs and the toys are a lot of fun. It also serves the purpose of nicely grounding participants who may have been doing something considerably more involved than a divination. The chance to eat a bit of chocolate and chuckle at the accuracy (or not) of the egg's contents provides a good laughter-banishing and closure for any heavy-duty ritual working.

We have received no prior inducements from Kinder to write this ritual, but a large free box of eggs wouldn't go amiss every month, if anyone from their management is reading....

Bigger, harder, faster, more… traffic signal servitors

The title is borrowed from a song by The The, a tune which emphasises how we all want more from the world, and we want it all NOW!

Drivers: wouldn't it be nice to be able to have the traffic signal lights change in your favour when you wanted? Yeah. Well, here's how to do it. Really.

In the latter half of the 1980s some companions and we were at a loose end one day, and we decided to create an experimental servitor (or thought-form) to do "something", since we had just devised a new and interesting method of creating them, and needed a function to assign to one. They are basically an artificially-created entity, to perform simple functions for the magician. A bit like a familiar, too.

Anyway, semantics are not important, servitors are basically magical robots that can be made, and, with care in the preparation, they can work well. The mechanics of our particular method are not important here, in any case, since we've done all that end of the work for you.

The important thing it to keep it simple: a servitor will do exactly what it is told, and literally at that; so if you were to make one to wash your clothes it might well just choose to flood your house, since that is one simple task (burst a pipe in your attic to release masses of water onto the clothing) rather than several complex and sequential tasks (pick up clothes, put in washing machine, add detergent, close washer door, press correct permutation of buttons). Not a great example, but it illustrates the problems - you need to think like a robot in order to design good ones.

Think of them as very small and stupid children with little sense of what is 'right and wrong' and no common sense, but who react well to both love and *carefully-phrased, simple instructions*.

So we talked for a while, and since we were mostly car drivers, we decided to try to make something to change traffic lights to green. Sounds too good to be true, right? Having some semblance of morality at the time (which has since happily vanished), we decided to programme in one 'check and balance', namely that no-one could abuse the servitor to make it change lights all the time; it would work best when the driver was in a genuine hurry, or if it was a medical emergency. At other times the servitor would not act unless it wanted to.

So, we devised a set of attributes based on the above requirements, and decided that the servitor would do nothing other than change traffic lights to green when asked, and providing the circumstances were of the requisite urgency.

Otherwise it was up to the Servitor as to whether to react, depending on the sincerity of the call to change the lights, or how hungry it was (see below). This allowed it to make a choice if two of us were approaching lights at the same 4-way junction, from different directions, as we did on occasion, just to see what happened. Invariably the most sincere and biggest hurry won out each time. We could have just told it to do as it was asked at all times, but that would be a miserable existence for the little beastie.

A name was devised, and a sigil constructed based on that name, with the entity being made with an intrinsic need to feed on a combination of green light and expressions of pleasure from drivers. In a ritual held inside a car parked on the kerb at a busy road junction (hell, we had such glamorous temples in those days...) the sigil was bathed in green light from a torch masked with some coloured cellophane, and many pleasurable words, in a mantra form, this act being to charge the sigil, and to bring the servitor to life. At the end of the ritual the sigil was sealed in a metal box lined with black paper, and that box was wrapped in several layers of opaque material.

It was later ritually buried in the bottom of a deep dark hole, under the impenetrable shade of a very ancient and massive Yew tree (an evergreen, thus with shade all year round) in the very middle of a deep, dark and silent forest in the south of England, very far from any roads, far from any noise and light. The servitor itself was set free, but commanded to listen out, to listen for those drivers who had created it calling its name, and to act according to the rubric given above.

We experimented with the servitor, and results were rather interesting, and very good. With practice at the correct intonation and attitude we were stopped by very few red lights on our journeys, the beastie fed well on a lot of green light, and on a lot of smiling drivers' vibes.

This success-rate continued for some months, until it got to the point where two of us very nearly had separate and very serious car crashes on the same day. We had become so much used to changing red lights at will that the physical "brake" reflex in our feet was becoming atrophied. Oh.

The servitor is not to be abused, and we had been doing that in our arrogance - we'd been driving around purely for fun at rapid speeds, just trying it out, and we presume it had become tired. So we cut back on use, and the success rate went up again. This was one sensible beastie we'd created; why tire yourself out all day when you can do a little work now and then, and remain quite well fed? Quite.

So, it carried on for year after year, with the original few of us using the Servitor just enough to keep it busy and well fed. In the first couple of years of the 21st Century, two of the original creators died. Not in car accidents, we hasten to add. But less of the original creators on the road means the beastie was not being used enough, and was getting hungry and bored. And so in a modification to the ritual we have allowed the servitor to breed.

Anyone who reads this and puts the servitor name into use as detailed below will have their own cloned copy of ours, to use for their own traffic light changing, and it is hoped that the servitor will thus be used sufficiently to maintain it in happy working order.

Some caveats:

This had not originally been tested outside the UK, so we had no idea if it would like the green traffic lights of other countries, but felt that it should do. A subsequent correspondent in the USA reports: **"I did a workshop on Car Magic at XXXXX [20] which we empowered your entity to work**

20 The event and locations concerned have been obscured to avoid identifying the writer.

in the US. I had had no luck using it here, although it worked fine for me last summer in London, so I reckoned we just needed to charge it more fully. Whatever we did worked, because that very evening, back in XXX, I was able to change two lights green! I felt very proud of myself!".

We can take no responsibility for any car accidents you have when using it. In any case, we doubt a law court will take you remotely seriously if you try blaming us....

The servitor changes traffic lights for drivers only, and only while they are in cars. It does not work for pedestrians who want a "walk now" light on road crossings, and it does not make any other lights, such as those on various other pieces of machinery turn green. (We've tried, hell, we've tried....)

Okay, having said that, here are the operational details: the Servitor's name is SQUILD. That rhymes with "filled". To activate it the first time there is no need to use the sigil, you need sit in your stationary car and say the name slowly; visualising a vivid green light filling your being. Smile. When you feel content that you have made yourself noticed to Squild, stop visualising, and start the engine. It is only necessary to do this once per driver, but if you have more than one vehicle we find it useful to do it for each of them.

When driving and coming up to a red light that you need to change, say out loud, rapidly, **"Squild! Squild! Squild!"** (As if you were shouting out "Fire!" as an urgent warning of danger to someone, or as if you are about to reach orgasm, if you are a 'screamer') while staring at the traffic lights, and smiling very hard and genuinely. Ignore the reactions of your passengers (if any) or other drivers or pedestrians if you have your window open....

See what happens.... But don't abuse it. As has been often said of chaos magic, being outside the normal rules and Judeo-Christian-derived ethics in Western society of itself creates a new, relevant and entirely practical set of standards of behaviour. This is one of them. Until such point as it is no longer needed.

Since the creation of Squild we were delighted to read of *Fotamecus*, which in terms of achieving general travel speed blows out little beast out of the water. You can look it up easily on the web, but the main links are below:

We would be very interested to hear how our dear Squild is getting along with other drivers; please email us (see flyleaf) with the subject line 'Traffic Servitor'. We ignore spam of the kind "can you get me a boy/girlfriend with your magical spells, please?" To answer that question, yes we can, but we choose not to - see the love spells section for more info on why not.

The story of *Fotamecus*, designed by the most talented magician Fenwick Rysen is to be found on the www.chaosmatrix.org website. Note it is ORG, not COM.

For info on a fascinating *Fotamecus* film project go to:
http://homepage.ntlworld.com/matt.lee7/fotamecus

This site is also the web homepage of the excellent printed chaos magazine *Razor Smile*, where a shorter version of this piece first appeared.

Cellphone sigils

In the same way that sigils are constructed and produced by reducing the words of one's desire into the constituent letters, cellphone/mobile phone keypads can be used to construct and cast a sigil. There are three methods:

The first method uses the numbers on the phone keypad. Reduce your sigilised desire to the constituent letters as described much earlier, then using those letters identify a series of numbers from the cellphone keypad (which are used for sending text messages). For example on our cellphone, a cheap Nokia, the number 5 is associated with the letters J, K and L.

Arrange these numbers into the format of a telephone number for your country, and dial that number to activate the sigil. If anyone answers, ask if you can speak to Austin, or Mr Spare (choose one, while smiling), wait for the response, politely apologise for dialling the wrong number, and hang up. The chances are that the number will *not* be a recognised telephone number, and you will instead get an automatic taped reply to that effect. In either case, the sigil is cast. Oh yes, to avoid any awkward subsequent situations with the person you called, use a dial-back blocking code when calling (it is 1471 in the UK). Easy, huh?

The second method is to use the constituent letters of the intent as a text message, and send that message to a telephone number also derived from the letters, using a numerical method similar to the Sudoku magic square described earlier.

A third method needs confederates in a magickal group, each with their own cellphone. Have them geographically arranged in a rough circle surrounding a magical target, at whatever distance suits; yards or miles.

Send the chosen sigilised text message around sequentially from one cellphone to the next one geographically, either clockwise (when viewed from above) or anticlockwise depending on the intent - anticlockwise is generally considered to be a reductive, binding matter, while clockwise is a facilitative, creative matter, until the target has been surrounded in a matrix of radio signals which are transmitting the sigil. Have everyone visualise this while you are all doing it, and then all leave the area at a pre-arranged time, laughing.

An additional technique is to use your car to draw a geographical sigil. Look closely on a map and find a route around the required area where you can drive 'in circles' without too much bother. Then using your car, make a few circuits of your target, concentrating fully on your intent. We once spent an entire (and very long) evening driving round a target in triangles of about a mile distant (triangles, due to the local road layout) chanting a sigilised mantra, and from what we heard later, the person concerned was certainly painfully aware that something very odd was going on....

Moral Panicke Workshoppe

The media generate moral panics, and magick (or witchcraft or Satanism) is often one of 'the usual suspects', when paedophiles, immigrants or terrorists are off the menu, that is. Mr. Crowley is regularly invoked by the press, usually on a 'slow news day', as the most evil man in the world who's spirit still leads us into dark deeds, and the usual inaccurate garbage is trotted out about 5 of his mistresses killing themselves due to his Satanism and trafficking with sundry demons, etc, with only a desperately tenuous link to the actual story of the day. Yawn.

We think it was Mark Twain who observed that **"man is the only animal that blushes, or needs to"**; and it is precisely this kind of imposed guilt and/or shame that the psychovampiric demon Miijarhaip feeds on[21].

By identifying, isolating and then attacking any sub-group of society an atmosphere of division and resentment can be quickly built up; and an easy scapegoat to blame a complex problem on is often utilised by the media and politicians.

The great and terrible fear generated in the early 1990s in Britain by the apparent sudden incidence of satanic child abuse was a cause of immense grief to hundreds of traumatised parents who had their children taken away and who were then abused, and in some cases assaulted by their neighbours, on the strength of what they were believed to have done.

After a long and detailed investigation it was found that none of the children had been abused. The whole scare had originated with a small group of fundamentalist Christians in the USA who had apparently started up a consultancy to train police and social workers from all over the world in detecting "abuse"; awarding their own impressive certificates to those trained. Having gained these dubious qualifications the trainees then went out looking for abuse; and with no little surprise (and the co-operation of some sensationalist reporting in the media) a huge number of "true" cases was rapidly found. The hidden agenda here was, of course, the boost

21 Media hype. For more material on the magical usefulness of the personification of social factors in order to be able to work with them better, see the various works by Ramsey Dukes, especially his fabulous Little Book of Demons.

to respectability of Fundamentalism; and to their very financially lucrative seminars and training courses.

Practising Ritual Satanists are, in the real world, a pretty rare breed (it can be immensely hard work, after all...), and child abuse is not part of their ritual curriculum. On a scale of religious groups implicated in child abuse they are well towards the low end. It is in fact the various Christian denominations that are statistically highest in the child abuse table; which the fundamentalists obviously kept very quiet at the time. This example illustrates just how easy it is to manipulate a good moral panic with no basis in objective reality.

So, why not start your own moral panic as a blind, creating a ritually 'sacrificed' *My Little Pony*, or a *Scooby Doo* toy inscribed with faux-runes and leaving it in a churchyard? This would be an interesting start. Draw the runes in what looks like blood - find something that dries to a brown colour, like mixed red and blue food dye with a little "PVA" (which stands for Poly Vinyl Aldehyde, we think) waterproof wood glue to make it turn tacky like recently-spilt blood. Don't use actual runes, which may accidentally spell out something, just pick some arcane-looking shapes. All product terms used are probably trademarks.

Both the sheer entertainment value and function of this would be to make fundamentalists look even sillier than they are, once the sinister found objects are reported to the media by them, and a crusade has been started and there is an uproar from the fundies about 'Satanists in our midst'.

You can then step in as an anonymous expert and write a letter debunking the apparent 'satanic ritual' for what it was, a joke to expose the fundamentalist experts as the ignorant clowns that they are.

What's in a name? Snobbery and Pronunciation in Magick **(an interlude from Kate Hoolu).**

There is Spell-casting and there is Spelling in magic: this piece was at least partially prompted by a couple of conversations and overheard remarks at some occult-y social events, and can be very useful for the chaos cunner to bear in mind when talking with other magickians.

There's a terrible snobbery about pronunciation in magick, isn't there? It almost reaches the point where you wonder if you can't say the name of something the 'right' way, then are you 'worthy' of doing magic or witchery or whatever it is?

I had always pronounced Crowley as "Crau- Lee", (rhymes with foul-ly) and by the time we found out it was (probably) more correct to say "Cro- Lee" (rhymes with holy) it was such a matter of habit it couldn't be changed unless I tried really hard. I am still working on it. And yet later on at one event, someone who had corrected us about our pronunciation of Aleister Crowley's name went into a long and supposedly impressive diatribe about the Book of Thoth; but they were pronouncing it like it is spelt, rather than the "correct" rendering of the Egyptian, which is "tar-hoot-teh" (or something similar), so I am are told.... But not by anyone who is old enough to have ever spoken Egyptian in pre-christian times, so I'm not sure how they can be so sure of themselves.

And of course there is Taoism, which may be pronounced "Dow-izm" by those in the know. Or "Doh-izm" (as in Homer Simpson). And oh my goodness, don't get into the magical terminology which comes from Yoga! According to some of the windbags I've heard, if you get a click, a wince, a blink or a sigh wrong in your lengthy repetitions of difficult polysyllabic words you are surely doomed to eternal hells.... The 'traditional' Wiccan festivals are another one to sort out who knows the 'right' way to say things: - I've heard about 6 versions of how 'Lughnasadh' should sound, and there is a definite split between "Sam-Hayne" and "Sow-Wayne" for Hallowe'en (spelt Samhain).

There was also the really funny female witch who was talking about Imbolc (which she always pronounced Immolc, the B being usually silent) while supermarket shopping, and she pronounced it *Immac* as we were walking down the feminine products aisle and saw the leg hair removal stuff bearing that trademark....

I believe it was the nutty old magical bat Dion Fortune who 'reverse-engineered' an old ritual found in some dusty manuscripts; eventually coming up with the impressive God-name of T'GATU (very HP Lovecraft!), only to discover it was a third-generation copy of something Masonic, and T'gatu was a phonetic attempt at saying the acronym for The Great Architect of The Universe.

And don't get me started on alleged "Reiki Masters" and their blathering versions of the language. It's tempting to ascribe a lot of this 'more grammatical than Thou' stuff to some very earthly and mundane class warfare or one-upmanship (one-upwomanship, more often) - it seems to belong often to the same kind of social situation where one compares the size of the fourth bedroom or the second car with dinner-party companions, and discusses the cost of educating young Tarquin and Jemima.

I think it was George Bernard Shaw who revised the spelling of "FISH", via the conventions of English pronunciation to actually be "GHOTI"

It goes like this: GH- the gh in enough, to give the F sound, O – the o from women to give the I sound and TI – the ti - from education to give the SH sound.

A funny tongue, for sure. And a funny thing to be discussing in magic- I'm reminded of some papers that a friend is researching, from the late 'King of the Witches' in Britain, Alex Sanders. Sanders was a very accomplished medium as well as being a witch and magician, and one of his regular channelled 'visitors' was a 17th Century cunning man called Nick Demdike. Compared to many of the angelic entities channelled by Sanders at other times, Demdike is a particularly earthy character, who would be damn refreshing company in some of the events I've been to lately. Old Nick's parting words after one mediumship session via Sanders were apparently **"If I come across any angels I'll fucking have 'em... they'll get the end of my stick"**.

Perfect. I can't see anyone in the modern pagan world correcting Old Nick if he pronounced something a bit different from the accepted norm for a god name or a witch festival name. Well, they'd only correct him the once, anyhow.

So, we can conclude that the English language is very flawed and magic names are not always 'correct' as they are read out phonetically. So who's right? So what? Who gives a flying fuck about that? Unless we missed something in Magick 101, isn't it intention that matters?

The possibilities of inventing your own traditional magickal path name, spelt like a mundane word but pronounced VERY differently should not have escaped you.

When talking about my own path I now use an innocent-looking (and entirely fabricated) word, but one which employs the double-d spelling (but which is pronounced as a throaty, coughing LTh-sound from the Welsh) plus some other linguistic freakeries for this purpose. Devise and practice your own one for use as a convenient shut-up technique if you insist on moving in the kind of 'neo-pagan knitting circle' world I've described above, it can cause even more consternation than claiming to be a Satanist, or so I've found.

Kate now exits the book, smiling.

Handy Hint:

Sigils can be painted onto skin using edible body paint, and then eaten off.

Slowly.

The route of the gnosis here would probably be quite easy to guess, and delicious fun to generate…

What's dragging you down?

This working can be performed in rivers, lakes and (at a push) a public swimming pool (if the lifeguard is not too attentive to what you will actually be doing), but it's better done in a fast-flowing river or in mama Ocean, and in a good wild surf, too, rather than a nice calm millpond sea, so there is some element of danger, and gnosis is thus easier to get to.

Be aware of the dangers inherent in overdoing the gnosis. Have someone to hand ready and able to pull you out if you take the work a touch too far, and arrange a 'dead-hand' signal to mark your internal state. This is simple, you instruct your assistant to do nothing until they see your hand drop, and you take to the water with one fist clenched above your head. If you lose consciousness your hand will of course drop, so you do not have to remember to make a signal.

So, what IS dragging you down? This rite can be used to remove blocks of whatever kind in your life. Formulate the problem, and formulate a sigil that is a realistic solution or improvement to the situation (even if that is an achievable part of an idealised entire solution). Make it into a mantra you can repeat, and take it to the water. Get into the water with your assistant on standby, and hold up your dead-hand signal. Submerge yourself and repeat the mantra as many times as you can without passing out - really push yourself on this. Use the gnosis of reaching the surface and taking in a huge breath to propel the sigil outwards, towards the problem. This is a risky enough endeavour as it is, so take the usual care with not swimming where there are red warning flags etc.

Once you have performed, this rite and survived the waters, make a cash donation to one of the emergency services, or even better one of the rescue charities involved with water.

The Magus Word

We are not a Magus, but for a brief period of great need and magickal urgency during 1994 we had to temporarily act 'as if' we were one, and both rapidly acquire and consistently use that level of power. During that time, as a by-product of the experience, a 'Magus Word' was received, and it is this:

Amalgamation

We have no idea of the relevance (if any) outside of the events within which we were required to be a Magus[22], but if anyone has the will to spend some time doing Kenneth Grant-style cabbala with that and get back to us (email address at front of book) we would be grateful and interested. We suspect there is some mileage to be had in looking at the Am-Al-Ga-Maat-Ion side of things (anyone who's into Mr. Grant and his numerological and linguistic manipulations will understand at least what we're driving at here, the rest will be totally mystified, which probably shows how magickal this is).

Being able to come up with such ambiguous and impressive Magical words, dripping with hidden mystery and latent power, or even on occasion to be able to channel some cryptic, vaguely disjointed and possibly meaningful words from sundry spirits or 'Hidden Masters' to the utter confusion of most persons present is actually a vital ability for a credible cunner.

While it is not remotely Low Sorcery or terribly useful in daily life, it underpins the magickal reputation as a whole if one is seen to be in touch with intimidatingly weird higher powers as well as being able to charm the warts off someone's nose.

22 Which may yet become a Novel, one day, but we have been saying that for over a decade.

Handy Hint:

A half-bottle of Absinthe can be an invaluable addition to the Cunner's knapsack, if only as something exotic and arcane with which to knock people out when they become tiresome company.

The behaviourally-conditioned memory of a good, or in this context, 'bad', Absinthe hangover in your target will deter them from hassling you too much in the future.

The quality of mercy is not strained... **that would account for it's inconsistency**

We've been reminded in conversation of a report from the news around 7 years ago: it concerned reports that sheep have been using daring 'Special Forces-style' military assault tactics to cross cattle grids to reach greener pastures, and these were being used to support a controversial biologist's radical theory on transmission of animal behaviour.

Sheep in the New Forest in England had been seen co-operating to get into gardens to eat the tastier foliage found there compared to the rough grazing on which they were being kept. Some laid down on the cattle grids, making a "bridge" to allow the others to cross, in much the same way that Army troops are trained to rapidly cross barbed wire when attacking an objective by one man simply throwing himself down to form a bridge for his comrades to run across at speed and attain control of their target.

The New Forest is not so far from the home of the UK Police version of the FBI - a collection of scientists etc who are based together at Bramshill in Hampshire to research national crimes. Maybe these sheep were escaped super-intelligent research sheep from there, or something... but since the 1980s, reports of similar behaviour have come from Blaenau Ffestiniog in North Wales and the Malmoehus region of Sweden, among other places. We assume that the sheep do not have access to email or the telephone to communicate this method between themselves....

Dr Rupert Sheldrake, a former research fellow at Cambridge University, said this kind of event may not be coincidence but evidence of "morphic resonance", by which creatures communicate the benefits of their experiences to others without direct contact - a kind of subconscious telepathy, if you will.

Most scientists regard the morphic resonance idea with suspicion. The most prestigious academic journal *Nature* once described Sheldrake's book on the subject as "fit for burning", which is a nice, balanced and objective Nazi view from the premier scientific publication (not) - and very reminiscent of what the Americans did to Wilhelm Reich [23].

But Sheldrake argues that evidence for the existence of a morphogenetic field effect is mounting. The most famous example is in small birds such as blue tits taking the foil off the top of milk bottles to get at the cream inside. The first record of this habit was reported from Southampton in 1921, and its spread was recorded at regular intervals from 1930 to 1947… accelerating and spreading to Sweden, Denmark and Holland, and with a world war within that period probably doing much to disrupt both bird breeding cycles and consistent milk deliveries. But tits do not usually venture far – a territory of 15 miles across is considered to be quite exceptional, and at no point is the sea between the U.K. and continental Europe this narrow…. Spooooky!

To add weight to Sheldrake's ideas it should be noted that the activity spread ACROSS species, as quickly-, other birds doing the same thing, and the geographical spread within each species was about as rapid as the tits too… which cannot be explained away by psychological learning models of simple observation and copying.

So, to put some magick into this, see what, if anything, you can teach your local wildlife - try putting out food in unusual, challenging, containers that entail them thinking in order to eat. The increase in nature-intelligence outside your door might have a morphogenetic effect on your human neighbours….

We have seen a young captive octopus in a zoo aquarium turn both a key in a lock and open a door handle on a container in order to get at the live crab dinner inside the box… and animals remember very well - the octopus took a matter of a few moments to open it the *second* time the box was presented… (come on down Mr. Lovecraft, your time is nigh).

Sheldrake says morphic resonance can also affect humans. The rise in people's scores in standardised IQ tests decade on decade could be seen to match his predictions, as could the rise in exam success rates: or both-either could be seen as a glitch in the statistics… in any case, IQ itself has a few problems, as a lot of the initial research is deeply flawed and fabricated

23 See www.orgone.org

- there is not room for it here, but look around on the net for the story of Sir Cyril Burt.

One wonders what the birds are doing now that people either don't have milk delivered so much, or it arrives in tough plastic containers.... Cue a blackbird armed with a penknife or a power drill, perhaps.... Which reminds us of the old joke, what do you call a Blackbird with a machine gun?

"Sir"

Yeah, morphic resonance is a bit of a weird one; it sounds real-world science plausible, but seems to rely at least in part on some sort of psychic transference; which scientists find hard to swallow... Sheldrake is renowned as a bit of a hippy (spot the power of pejorative labelling), so 'finds it easier to deal with'... We try to keep an open mind, but it is a very compelling idea, and fits in with a lot of magical theories about how a 'link' is made and utilised when spellcasting....

Much useful magical material can be learned by using this in one or both of two ways. A morphic rite can be constructed to get in touch with a power animal that has learned to use tools - like creating a pathworking and invoking the intelligence of animals like the birds who have learned to use thorns to pick snails out of their shells, perhaps. Such capacity for innovation, when contacted and translated to human activities, is totally breathtaking in effect and implication; if this is carried through hard enough you could tune in to the morphic fields of the cleverest creatures (human and animal) on the planet....

An alternative method is to initiate a novel non-verbal behaviour change in yourself (something you desire other people to do), and repeat it in front of people, in a positive setting. In a short time, they will start repeating your actions. Technically that is not morphic resonance, it is behavioural conditioning, but fuck it, if it spreads useful actions then that's all we're bothered about.

Dr Sheldrake's material on this and many other fascinating subjects can be found at www.sheldrake.org.

Intents and Intensity

When tailoring spells to suit targets, try to ensure you are not giving them exactly what they don't need, for example one of the worst uses of magick (and your valuable time) would be to turn a current Wiccan spokesperson into a publicity-seeking egotist or similar.

A slight ethical consideration which might spring to mind as a critique of the more malefic aspects of this book could be along the lines of 'wouldn't it be better to cast spells to make people evolve out of their perceived bad state into something better?'

Yes it would, but it is much more work, and takes a lot longer, if you want quick results, go for the easiest target spell; which is usually the one that brings the faster relief to yourself, regardless of the effects on the other person or persons involved. We leave it to everyone else out there (who are, obviously, saints and perfected beings) to make the world a 'better place' with 'no evil, only pure light'.

A plug for Mr Crowley

Foreword to The 2002 Occult E-Books online edition of the Book of the Law, by Francis Breakspear

This is a book that is 'Biblical'. Not in length - in fact it may be one of the shortest Holy books ever written in any faith. But in scope? Sure. Reams have been written, and will yet be written about how it was received/composed/created by Crowley; what he had for breakfast that morning and what colour socks he was wearing, and most of that is fascinating, if only for the diligence of researchers, the beauty of the philosophical interpretations and the sheer entertainment value of some of the wilder theories. But what of the book, and what the hell is that little red book actually FOR?

This is an epic book, an awesome book, and an awe-full book. The shortest epic ever written and bears an author's name to strike fear into the heart of every fundamentalist Christian you could meet. That alone makes it worthwhile, and worth carrying on your person at all times, to produce like a hand grenade when needed. But there is far, far more to the book.

A book that was written by an upper-class Victorian rebel about dialogues with ancient Egyptian Gods from millennia before, but which finds resonance in part with a diverse band of modern magicians, witches, anarchists, artists, poets and musicians; and yet a book that no-one seems to entirely agree with. Such was Crowley: not a 'fluffy' new-age teacher to give anyone an easy ride, and determined to force them to think for themselves.

And think damned hard. Working with Uncle Aleister is like trying to arm-wrestle an octopus; there will always be something you can't quite get a handle on, and just when you think you've found a way - the whole beast turns to smoke and eludes you, until next time.

The Book of the Law is approaching a hundred years old, and forecast the cataclysmic decline of modern civilisation, the onset of an age of force, fire and war, and the rise of Horus as the God-form of this world. Pretty good. And pretty fresh for nearly 100. It was also the catalyst for Crowley's own world vision of a religion based on scientific approaches and is highly individualistic - you do what THOU wilt, after all. And that IS the greatest of great works- finding what thou wilt, and doing it; regardless of the innumerable social moralities and personal foibles and excuses which will get in the way, time after time. Never easy, always a challenge and the great task of our times.

The rituals of the old time are black, as is all else from the past. Purge, purge, purge and arise into a new Aeon, carrying only what you truly need, leaving behind the dross of what has been before. The seeming honour to write this introduction to the new edition of a Holy book is an illusion, but the chance to work with Crowley's techniques and adapt them to mine own will (and you, yours) is something more than honour. Generations as yet unborn will know and learn to love this book, containing as it does one functional means for the ultimate liberation of the human spirit.

Did WE say biblical? But not in the same enslaving way as that large tome tends to do: follow the Bible or Book of the Law by rote and you're in deep trouble, but open your mind to the meaning behind the metaphor in Liber Al, and work with it and you are standing on the runway, waiting for the flight to the Stars. So take up the sword and the wand, and what a flight it is!

This intro needs to stop here; learning one lesson from Liber AL: keep it short and let the reader do the work themselves. Work, endure and succeed. Success is your proof!

The Book of the Law as a Sacramental

The mighty yet compact book is a very handy and portable text for the Cunner to carry at all times, to impress the masses. It can be downloaded for free at www.occultebooks.com, and various other places. Try using printed-out pages from that in the same way that old-school cunners employed pages from the Bible as sacramentals - either randomly wrapping pieces around wounds or laying them on parts needing healing, or actually reading the thing and making up an index of suitable verses tailored for healing purposes and suchlike.

The book contains some simply beautiful imagery (in-between the violence) and can be of great use for this kind of task.

The Law is for All.

And for all purposes.

Handy Hint:

If you think you are being followed or observed when you go outdoors in rural areas to do ritual, to create a blind for sites where you work your real magic, take the time to leave 10-foot diameter rings of flour, soot, ash, dirt, sugar, salt etc in 'diversion' areas not too near to your actual working spot. No-one in their right mind will cross these obviously spooky sites, or even go near them, that being the benefit of living on a very superstitious planet....

Another good camouflage is to go to your local church sometimes, smile pleasantly, and sing the hymns at least as well and as loudly as the other people in the congregation and leave a reasonably generous donation in the plate when it passes. Having previously urinated or spat on the coins and allowed them to dry off, of course.

Nightmare Catchers

You will have probably seen dream-catchers in many a new-age shop? A circle of wire, bound with some suede or leather, coloured threads in a spider-web arrangement, with perhaps a few desultory beads and limp feathers hanging below. Sold for silly money. They are supposed to, if hung in a bedroom, catch the bad dreams that might assail your sleep.

Very 'ethnic', and very 'stolen wholesale from another tradition'. I wonder what the modern native Americans dream of at night nowadays, after a recent few hundred years' history of invasion, genocide, environmental rape, forced marches and exile from their tribal lands.... They dream of having enough to eat and not having to deal with mass unemployment and endemic alcoholism, probably, now that their lands are fundamentally screwed up by the white man.

So why only catch dreams? What about the real fucking nightmares? And the pursuit dreams, as discussed above. This is a design for a nightmare catcher:

You will need: some florists' wire, some coloured threads, fishing hooks, a razor blade, some dexterity and a deal of patience.

Wind the wire tightly around the base of a bottle several times, until you have a circle.

Tie the wire off to itself and remove from the bottle. This is the 'bones' of your nightmare catcher. Carefully bind the wire with coloured threads, tinsel, string, more wire etc, until it is aesthetically vaguely unpleasant in appearance. Now make a web in the centre of the ring, using more thread, just like a standard dream catcher. Adorn with some barbed fishing hooks and slip the razor blade into the centre using a short length of wire. Add any personal touches such as bone fragments, human teeth etc, to suit your own taste.

To charge the catcher, prepare a short ritual where, in your own words you address the catcher, tell it what you want it to do (catch your nightmares) and use the razor blade to take a small quantity of your blood and anoint the catcher with it, to seal the Pact and feed the Catcher. Hang the nightmare catcher high over your bed, and sleep peacefully thereafter.

To work a more particular and specific kind of magick with this, a photograph or some other token of another person who is causing you headaches can be hung on one of the fishing hooks, with the hook piercing their face if you are using a photograph, to divert your nightmares to them. If left hanging for long enough this really can, and will, coincide with people going quite insane.

Handy Hint:

With intent, cut a stem from a thorned rose, about half an inch thick and at least 18 inches long. Remove the thorns from the first few inches at one end (to make a handle). Paint the whole thing black.

When dry this will perform very well as a magick wand for works of restriction, removal of beauty and joy, literal 'deflowering' of someone's dreams etc, and it can be used to beat on a poppet with some useful effects.

Also, sigils can be drawn on balloons, which are then inflated. Go around the balloons with this wand, bursting them and thus setting them off into action- as with the sound of breaking glass, a bursting balloon is a powerful behavioural signal.

While we are talking wands, an instant and portable wand can be made from a car (automobile) telescopic radio antenna.

A Suffix on Ethics

We have particularly taken the angle from a magickal perspective. It's not a 'moral high ground from which to judge the herd mentality' as some egotistical mages and gurus would have it, rather it is just a different perspective, and probably equally skewed as any other.

So rather than pontificate, we decided here to include a selection of what contemporary Chaos magicians and a few others think about the whole good-evil shebang, and threw in some of our own thoughts, for people to choose their own meanings and standards. Again, this is not a comfortable read: turn back here if easily offended.

Still here? OK - the traditional 'third warning', as given in some initiatory schools: this is not a remotely 'fluffy' section; it's very nasty in places, proceed by your own will and your own acceptance of the consequences....

The magician is fully aware of, and actively, amorally utilises the fact, popularised by the great Robert Anton Wilson[24] that 'you know how dumb the average bloke is, right? Well by definition half of the bastards are dumber than THAT!". In other words, there are a lot of sheep out there to be fleeced, depending on the ingenuity and intent of the operator - i.e. if you are a "bad person" or not, or if your "morals" are "suspect"....

"The toxick magician is not the cause of human suffering. Human suffering is the norm". Hyatt, Psychopath's Bible, p 78. (Hyatt uses the term Toxick Magician for something analogous to a chaos magician, someone who is without conventional morality and playing the game entirely for the individual).

This is a stance taken in some forms of Buddhism, too.

And just how do you measure fear? Our friend Kate Hoolu suggests: "there is no reliable unit of measure of fear (although decibels of scream has been suggested!)".

24 www.rawilson.com. He was still alive when we wrote this, but apparently fading fast. Gods speed, Bob.

Intent is a big factor in questions of good and evil. As the saying goes, a knife is neutral, you can use it to stab someone to death or perform life-saving surgery. Same knife, could even be the same person using it, just on different days, different intent, different outcome. Try to imagine walking around in the street openly bearing a knife, either dressed in street clothes or magical robes and think what might happen when the cops turn up. Even someone in operating theatre garb openly carrying a scalpel on the street just a short distance from a hospital is going to stir up some public disquiet, and generate the sound of police sirens pretty rapidly.

And of course there are all the moral dilemma-thought experiments: "suppose you can travel back in time and kill Hitler, would you do it?"

Try that one on a fluffy, pacifist friend... ha ha.

More complex matters arise... the 'traditional' Wiccan dogma[25] is words to the effect of "providing it harms no-one, do what thou wilt"... which is fine up to a point, but although we are no shade of Wiccan we like to add the codicil of "unless it's in self-defence, then anything goes, and then it's a case of the last one left standing wins, motherfuckers"- ... this attitude has upset a few of our fluffier witchy friends (but, tellingly, these are precisely the same ones who always come to us when there is some piece of magick required that is necessary for their ends, but at best a little 'grey' in aspect, so their stupid and dogmatic public morals won't let them actually do it for themselves...) defining self-defence is also a moot point - especially when it comes to pre-emptive, preventative actions.

And of course the tabloid public perception is that we are all evil anyway - that magic is black, black, black... and if it's in the papers, it must be true, right?

Nature is not 'evil' as such. Nature has no morals (they being a human construct), and the standard example, often given, of the supposed "cruelty" of nature is those species of wasps who lay their eggs in the heads of other insects; debilitating to, but not killing them, so that when the babies hatch out they have a live meal waiting for them. The wasp has no concept of good or bad, it is just providing for the children....

25 'Traditions' form very rapidly, obviously.

Everyone has a dark side; which must be acknowledged. In some, ourselves possibly included, it is often their BETTER side....

We are conscious that this is precisely the morality section we weren't going to write, but heck... we weren't initially sure if we wanted to promote something, this book, that could increase the power of potential manipulators out there. We all do it at times of course, but this book is a manual of techniques that will make life a lot more interesting, and if purposively employed, will give you some increased degree of daily power over the world, and those people within it.

This may or may not be a morally 'right' thing to do on a societal level, depending on your stance on such matters. You might calm yourself by thinking of it as a very useful self-defence manual, and bear in mind the Tar baby story.

What happens if two people who have this book go at each other for all they are worth? Messy. If you find yourself in such a situation it may well be the fastest piece of results magick to simply not play the game, and do something more interesting and productive in any case.

We should also remark that while we have provided plenty of material in here that could be used for cursing, we have specifically not provided *everything* we know and use, and we have automatic and effective protection in place should anyone be numbskullish enough to try to use our own methods against us. You don't last this long in this game without being able to do at least that....

"Despite the glamour, Chaos magicians are rarely completely amoral. One of the basic axioms of magical philosophy is that morality grows from within, once you have begun to know the difference between what you have learned to believe, and what you will to believe." (Phil Hine, Oven Ready Chaos, p 45).

Handy Hint:

Draw a sigil on paper, wrap it around brick or large stone and throw it through a pane of glass with great force.

Obviously, doing that to a window that is not your property is not so sensible, as you may lay yourself open to criminal charges.

There is no reason, however, why you cannot do this in a setting where it is 'allowed', such as a demolition site, in a dumpster or builder's skip or with a pane of your own glass taken from a window that has been refitted.

The glass does not have to be an actual window for a very powerful gnosis to happen, so heavily are we conditioned to the sound of the stuff breaking....

Exorcisms and House-Clearance

Most of the time this comes more under 'pagan social work' than actually fighting with nasty spirits, as to perform house-cleansing rites is pretty common when there is no actual magical need to do so, but it makes people feel better about their new home, which is not contaminated in any way by spirit, but merely a strange new environment. Easy job, and good for the reputation, so if that is your taste, do them every time you are asked.

Be more circumspect about tales of weird happenings in houses that need to be exorcised though. Often times it is just noisy thought forms, and sometimes it is entirely benevolent spirits who just want to be heard, so exorcising them is the ultimate in bad manners - listen to what is going on in the house before you do anything to banish it.

We did a 'house exorcism' - in the 80s, not a full-on demon removal, but there was some pretty crappy thoughtform debris in that house that was centred around a young woman with some mental problems, injection drug issues, huge relationship troubles and a desperately clinging new involvement with Wicca in an attempt to solve her problems, while the particular Wiccans she got involved with were actually doing her more damage with their approach to the issue, ascribing it to karma and both not wishing to do anything to help and denying that there was any way that anyone else *could* help....

We were asked via her mother to come in and do some formal ritual to clean up the vibe - very much a 'set the clocks back to zero' cleansing operation, lots of chucking salt around, consecrated water, inscribing protective sigils on each window and doorstep with incense ash, chanting, ritual licences to depart for trapped spirits, the full-on 'traditional' ceremonial high magick package.

It wasn't a very pleasant experience, as some of it certainly was uncleared debris from invocations and suchlike, and that tends to "rot" if it hangs around, we find, and there was an exhausting and dirty scuffle in the general vibe of the building when it came time to remove the crud... and once it was done we were immediately moved to remark, off the cuff, in a faux-American radio announcer accent:

"Elv-es have left the building!"

We suppose it's a kind of banishing with laughter... it worked anyhow, the place and the occupants settled down hugely after that.

Degradation-Sigil Banishing

An old 'by degradation' means of banishing a problem was to sigilise the nature of it and draw that in chalk on the inside face of your chimney, and then to start a fire in the grate, so that the soot produced by the fire would over time obscure the sigil.

Nowadays there are fewer chimneys to be had with the advent of central heating etc., so a small sigil drawn on a cigarette, which is then lit but not smoked, but left in an ashtray to burn down to the butt can have a similar banishing effect. Alternately, draw it on the side of a candle and allow it to burn down, so the drawn sigil is vaporised over time.

While talking of sooty things, if there is something of a magical intent that you wish to 'take into yourself' then it can of course be sigilised onto a cigarette that is smoked by you.

A Square Meal Curse

Steal a small plate or cup from the kitchen of the person you wish to bewitch. Steal it carefully, and subtly, as with the footwear example given much earlier. This is a very personal link, being the vehicle by which they have on occasions received their vital bodily nourishment.

We leave it up to the individual magickian to work out how very debilitating a well-crafted and executed ritual smashing of (with intent), or urinating/defecating onto (ditto), such a route of nourishment could be upon the target. Repeating the latter acts daily would add to the potential debilitating effects.

Alternatively, steal a fork and ritually bend it into a hideously contorted and useless (at least useless for eating) shape. Discard it, ritually, into deep water, preferably very deep, cold and inhospitable muddy water, with intent.

Afterword

This small book has been in part an attempt to put some varied modern cunning chaos techniques into print, and into wider use, as we are obviously not going to live forever and can only teach them to a limited number of folk in person.

It's your own responsibility how you use this material. There are many techniques that are of no fixed moral purpose. A lot of loathsome Wiccans that we know will hate this book, no doubt, which is a bonus, as we find their fluffy-Fascism equally distasteful. Cursing is evil, but what if you are cursing one person to protect a thousand....

Magic can harm or heal, depending on the intent of who is doing the magic, so however you choose to wield the wand on each occasion, please at least do it well, with flair, style and grace....

Magic should also be **WILD**

Real magic, that is; not the sanitised stuff now being peddled as magic by the all-stifling, spreading neo-Church of the pop-pagan equivalent of the Womens' Institute.... Substitute chakra-candle workshops for jam-making and they are not so different, twig?

The best magic is not neat and tidy with large-print laminated scripts given out to all beforehand, and *ad nauseam* ritual rehearsals that suck every last atom of joy and soul from the process. It is 'dirty', it is messy, it comes from within, spontaneously, and explosively, and it is this kind of magic that we have tried to describe here. Ironically in the process of description and organizing chapters it has had, to an extent, to be sanitised, contained, punctuated and made less spontaneous.

Oh well. Get out there and get wild and dirty with the ideas, please!

We hope you enjoyed it, and as a last ritual, we can only suggest you run down to the sea (or to a river, a lake or even a puddle), pick up the biggest rock you can find, inscribe it with a simple sigil, like your own fingerprint, impressed in your own spit, and throw it as far out into the water (or as hard into the puddle) as you can, and screaming out :

**" F U U U U U U U U U U U U U U U U U U U U U U U U U U U U U U U -
U U U U U U U U U U U U U U U U U U U U U U U U U U U U U U U U -
UUUUUUUUUUUUUUUUUUUUCK IIIIIIIIIIIII
AAAAAAAAAAAAAAAAAAMMMMMMMMMMMMMM
AAAAAAAAAAAAAAAALLLLLLLLLLLLLLLIIIIIIIIIIIIIIIIIV-
VVVVVVVVVVVVVVVEEEEEEEEEEEE !!!!!"**

as loudly as you possibly can. When it hits the water, run away laughing hysterically, and then immediately go do something else entirely. And whatever you do, do not look back.

You could also substitute this book for the rock, of course.

If you have successfully taken on any of the ideas here and made them work, and especially if you have usefully developed them further using your own skills, you are now a fully-fledged and initiated new traditional Chaos Cunner and Urbane Shaman.

Now **that's** what we call gnosis....

Recommended Sources

Francis likes these people, you might do too:

Professor Ronald Hutton, Ramsey Dukes -aka Lionel Snell- aka quite a few other names, see www.occultebooks.com and his numerous fab books, the late Stephen J Gould, Phil Hine, Owen Davies, the late Andrew Chumbley, Julian Vayne, Greg Humphries, Jaq Hawkins, the delicious Kate Hoolu, Dave Lee, Peter Carroll, Terry Pratchett, Robert Anton Wilson, Clive Barker.

Editors' Notes

We should tell the reader who has made it this far that Francis Breakspear often wishes he was merely a convenient fiction, but while he is sometimes far more real than he thinks he should be, he has trouble with consensus reality at the best of times. He is often not sure if someone 'else' is 'writing him'; which gets him into all sorts of painful and ultimately irresolvable Cartesian gymnastics.

You may notice that this book is largely written without employing the individual personal pronoun (apart from in any quotes from other people) - this is deliberate, for those reasons.

We would have done an index, but it seemed (a) too nerdy, (b) simply an opportunity to waste some more paper, and (c) if we had done it then it would have been done mischievously, like this:

The spell about audiotape ..... page 7
The spell about audio CDs ..... page 24

etc... and so we decided that our time would be better spent going out into the world to take our manifold and immense joys in being both cunning and urbane, and that choice of action would make it faster, or at least more fun to finally reach.

an end

May some or other deity (which may or may not exist in any case) bless most of you.

Email us (see flyleaf) to go on the 'notify list' for new titles. Thanks.

Aleister Crowley and the 20th Century synthesis of Magick

"Strange distant Gods that are not dead today"

by Dave Evans

Both a professional academic researcher and practising magician, Dr Dave Evans delves into modern history to present a serious, but accessible and fascinating work, based on research work done for a Master of Arts degree on the history and literature of British magic, focussing especially on Aleister Crowley.

Topics covered include Aleister Crowley and Thelema, Dennis Wheatley, Kenneth Grant, Jack Parsons, Tom Driberg, the British spying community, Austin Osman Spare, Gerald Gardner and others.

Being a useful biography of Crowley, plus more, this accessible and diverse book can be considered a prequel of, and a seed for the author's larger subsequent volume The History of British Magic After Crowley.

ISBN 978-0-9555237-2-4 published by Hidden Publishing
original e-book published by el-cheapo books

For more details, go to
WWW.OCCULTEBOOKS.COM

The History of British Magic After Crowley

Kenneth Grant, Amado Crowley, Chaos Magic, Satanism, Lovecraft,
The Left Hand Path, Blasphemy and Magical Morality

by Dave Evans

Dr Dave Evans delves deeply into modern British history to present a serious, but accessible and fascinating work, based on his recent and unique PhD, on developments in British magic after Aleister Crowley died. Not just the result of extensive book-research, this project involved attending rituals and having meetings with some quite remarkable men and women, who are examined and given a voice in these pages, some of them for the first time.

Topics covered include Aleister Crowley and Thelema, How many magicians there actually are in Britain, The claims of Amado Crowley to be Aleister's son, the work of Austin Osman Spare, Kenneth Grant and the Typhonian OTO, Blasphemy, Chaos Magick, Gerald Gardner, Ramsey Dukes, Alex Sanders, HP Lovecraft, Satanism, Cursing, The Left-Hand Path, creating the Journal for the Academic Study of Magic, plus the work of Ronald Hutton, Dennis Wheatley, Dion Fortune, HP Blavatsky and others, all meshed into a broader philosophical, cognitive-psychological and moral-history framework of the broader Twentieth Century.

Not just a book about the history of magic, this research places magicians and their work into the broader society that we all live in, and shows how that magic has always been a part of our culture.

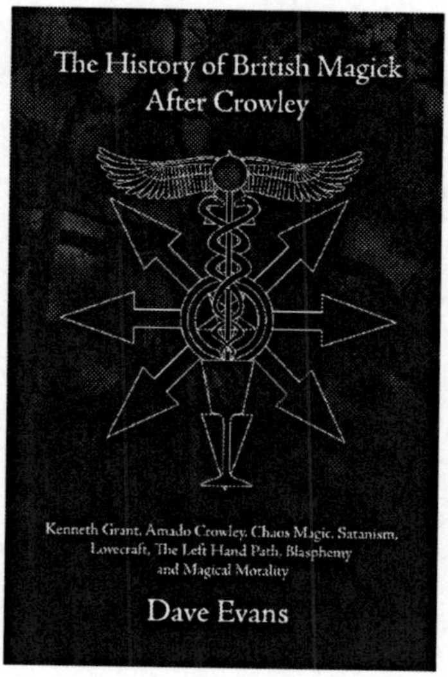

ISBN 978-0-9555237-0-0 published by Hidden Publishing

The Journal for the Academic Study of Magic (JSM)

A multidisciplinary, peer-reviewed print publication, covering all areas of magic, witchcraft, paganism etc; all geographical regions and all historical periods.

Issue 1

Alison Butler - Beyond Attribution: The Importance of Barrett's Magus • John C. Day - Shadow over Philistia: A review of the Cult of Dagon • Joyce Goggin - A History of Otherness:Tarot and Playing Cards from Early Modern Europe • Dave Green - Opposites Attract: magical identity and social uncertainty • Matt Lee - 'Memories of a sorcerer': notes on Gilles Deleuze-Felix Guattari, Austin Osman Spare and Anomalous Sorceries. • Ilaria Serra - Le Streghe Son Tornate: The Reappearance of Streghe in Italian American Queer Writings • Deana Weibel - Controlling Chance, Creating Chance: Magical Thinking in Religious Pilgrimage

Issue 2

JustinWoodman - Alien Selves: Modernity and the Social Diagnostics of the Demonic in 'Lovecraftian Magick' • Dave Green - Wishful Thinking Notes towards a psychoanalytic sociology of Pagan magic • Vanessa Chambers - A Shell with my Name on it: The Reliance on the Supernatural During the First World War • Morgan Luck - The Metaphysical Relationship between Magic and Miracles • Jason Semmens - Demonic Possession, and Spiritual Healing in Nineteenth-Century Devon • Andria Filipovic and Anne M. Rader - Human Body in Southern Slavic Folk Sorcery • Lionel Snell - Four Glasses Of Water • Amy Hale - The Land Near the Dark Cornish Sea • Dave Evans - Kenneth Grant and the Magickal revival • Aaron Cheak - Magic through the Linguistic Lenses of Greek mágos, Indo-European *mag(h)-, Sanskrit màyà and Pharaonic Egyptian heka • Joyce Froome - The symbolism of the pierced heart• John McCannon - Shamanic Motifs in Fin-de-Siecle Russian Art: The Case of Nicholas Roerich

Issue 3

Hannah Sanders - Buffy and Beyond: Language and Resistance in Contemporary Teenage Witchcraft • Amy Lee - A Language of Her Own: Witchery as a New Language of Female Identity• Dave Green - Creative Revolution: Bergsonisms and Modern Magic • Mary Hayes - Discovering the Witch's Teat: Magical Practices, Medical Superstitions in The Witch of Edmonton • Penny Lowery - The Re-enchantment of the Medical: An examination of magical elements in healing. • Jonathan Marshall - Apparitions, Ghosts, Fairies, Demons and Wild Events: Virtuality in Early Modern Britain • Kate Laity - Living the Mystery: Sacred Drama Today • Research Articles: David Geall - 'A half-choked meep of cosmic fear' Is there esoteric symbolism in H.P.Lovecraft's The Dream-Quest of Unknown Kadath? • Susan Gorman - Becoming a Sorcerer: Jean-Pierre Bekolo's Quartier Mozart and the Magic of Deleuzian and Guattarian Becoming • Book Reviews

Issue 4 - out soon   Issue 5 - due for publication late 2007

Further details about the journal can be found at the SASM website: www.sasm.co.uk

Lightning Source UK Ltd.
Milton Keynes UK

171769UK00001B/65/A

9 780955 523717